J. J. WALLACE

Personal Finance for Beginners to Master Money Skills

An Essential Guide to Budget and Manage Money Wisely

Contents

Introduction

Welcome to Personal Finance for Beginners: How to Budget and Manage Your Money Wisely. In today's fast-paced world, financial literacy is more crucial than ever. Whether you are just starting in your job, trying to pay off debt, or planning for retirement, mastering money skills is critical to establishing financial stability and long-term success.

This book is intended to provide you with the information and practical tools needed to handle the intricacies of personal finance. It offers a step-by-step approach, providing simple explanations and valuable suggestions to help you create good money management habits.

Throughout this book, you will find a wealth of information that is both informative and motivational. We'll look at common misconceptions about personal finance, the importance of having a healthy financial mindset, and how to develop SMART financial goals. Each chapter builds on the preceding one to provide a thorough grasp of personal finance, covering everything from budgeting and tracking income and expenses to saving, debt management, and investing methods.

What sets this book apart is its participatory and reflective nature. Those informative chapters will help you comprehend and reflect on your own experiences. You will also have access to extra resources such as suggested books, websites, and tools for lifelong learning.

It's important to note that personal finance is not a one-size-fits-all solution. Each person has distinct circumstances and aspirations that necessitate personalized tactics. This book provides a conceptual overview and theoretical analysis of many financial problems and the skills you need to apply these principles to your situation.

This book combines current personal finance trends with historical context to help you understand how cultures have shaped financial institutions throughout time. In addition, we base our suggestions on scientific research and data-driven insights.

Personal finance might be complicated, but this book strives to demystify issues with short, accessible language forms and vivid descriptions. We allow readers to absorb the knowledge without feeling overwhelmed by presenting it at a regulated pace. We aim to empower readers by providing practical answers they can adopt right now.

Personal finance is more than just collecting wealth; it's about living without financial stress. By taking control of your finances, you can experience better peace of mind, pursue your aspirations, and have the freedom to make decisions consistent with your principles.

So, let us go on this adventure together, where we will demystify personal finance and provide you with the tools you need
to master money skills. Prepare to transform your financial
future and unlock your full potential. Remember, every step
forward leads to a brighter, more financially secure future.

Chapter 1: Why Personal Finance Matters

"Money, like emotions, is something you must control to keep your life on the right track." - Natasha Munson

Natasha's quote highlights the importance of mastering money skills to maintain control over our lives. Just as we need to manage our emotions to make sound decisions and lead fulfilling lives, we must learn how to control our finances to achieve stability, security, and financial well-being.

Personal finance is not just about balancing a checkbook or paying bills on time; it encompasses many skills and knowledge that can empower us to make informed decisions about our money and create a secure financial future.

In this chapter, we will explain why personal finance matters and how it can profoundly impact our overall well-being. We will debunk common misconceptions about personal finance, learn how to overcome fears around managing money and discover the importance of setting goals for financial success. Together, we will take the first steps towards financial independence, armed with the confidence and knowledge needed to navigate the complex world of personal finance.

1.1 The Importance of Financial Literacy in Today's World

Financial literacy has become more crucial in today's fast-paced and ever-changing world. Understanding personal finance and mastering money skills are essential for individuals to navigate the complexities of modern life and achieve long-term financial success.

Financial literacy refers to the knowledge and skills necessary to make informed decisions about money management, budgeting, investing, and debt management. It empowers individuals to take control of their finances, make sound financial choices, and plan for a secure future.

With financial literacy, individuals may avoid financial pitfalls such as excessive debt, poor credit scores, and inadequate savings. They may also need help to meet their basic needs or face difficulties achieving their financial goals.

Moreover, financial illiteracy can have broader societal impacts. It perpetuates income inequality, hinders economic growth, and contributes to financial instability. By lack of understanding of personal finance, individuals may fall into cycles of poverty and struggle to break free from it.

By acquiring knowledge about personal finance and developing strong money management skills, individuals can build a solid foundation for their financial well-being. They can gain confidence in making informed decisions about spending, saving, investing, and borrowing wisely.

Financial literacy provides individuals the tools to set realistic financial goals and develop actionable plans. Whether saving for a down payment on a home, starting a business, or planning for retirement, understanding personal finance is essential for success.

Furthermore, financial literacy equips individuals with the skills to navigate the complexities of an increasingly digital and interconnected economy. With technology revolutionizing our finances, it is crucial to understand concepts such as online banking, digital payments, and cybersecurity to protect personal information and assets.

1.2 Common Misconceptions about Personal Finance

Understanding personal finance is essential for gaining control over one's financial life and achieving long-term financial success. However, several common misconceptions often hinder people from effectively managing their money. So, we will debunk these misconceptions and provide you with the knowledge needed to overcome them.

Misconception 1: "I don't have enough money to start managing my finances."

One of the biggest misconceptions about personal finance is that it only applies to people with substantial wealth. However, the truth is that everyone, regardless of their income level, can benefit from understanding and practicing good financial habits. Starting early and implementing little changes allows even people with minimal resources to progressively improve their financial status and pave the path for a brighter future.

Misconception 2: "Financial management is complicated and time-consuming."

Another common misconception is that managing personal finances requires expertise in complex financial concepts and a significant amount of time. While it's true that financial management involves some level of knowledge and effort, it doesn't have to be overwhelming or overly time-consuming. Anyone may learn how to manage their money successfully by breaking it down into small steps and using the available tools and resources.

Misconception 3: "I can rely on someone else to handle my finances."

Many believe they can delegate their financial responsibilities to others, such as family members, financial advisors, or even the government. While seeking professional advice is beneficial, it's essential to recognize that you are ultimately responsible for your financial well-being. Actively managing your funds gives you control and empowerment over your financial decisions.

Misconception 4: "Budgeting restricts my freedom and enjoyment."

Some people look at budgeting as limiting their freedom to spend money on things they enjoy. However, budgeting is not about restricting yourself but allocating your resources wisely to prioritize what truly matters to you. Creating a budget based on your objectives and desires allows you to make deliberate decisions consistent with your beliefs and gets you closer to financial freedom.

Misconception 5: "I'm too young to worry about personal finance."

Many young adults believe that personal finance is something they can worry about later in life when they have more stability or higher income. However, establishing good financial habits early on can set the foundation for a lifetime of financial success. The power of compounding interest makes saving and investing from an early age immensely valuable.

1.3 The Impact of Personal Finance on Overall Well-being

Personal finance plays a crucial role in determining our overall well-being. When we control our finances, we experience greater peace of mind, reduced stress, and improved mental and emotional health. On the other hand, financial instability can lead to anxiety, sleepless nights, and strained relationships.

One of the critical aspects of personal finance is having a solid financial foundation. Individuals can establish a strong foundation for their future by mastering money skills and making intelligent financial decisions. This foundation provides a sense of security and allows us to confidently navigate life's uncertainties.

Financial stability also allows us to pursue our passions and dreams. By managing our money wisely, we can invest in personal and professional growth opportunities that align with our values and goals. Whether it's starting a business, traveling the world, or supporting causes we care about, having control over our finances enables us to make choices that enhance our well-being and bring fulfillment.

Moreover, personal finance directly impacts our physical well-being. Financial struggles can lead to neglecting important areas of self-care, such as maintaining a healthy diet or seeking necessary medical attention. We can better prioritize our health and participate in activities that enhance overall wellness if we manage our money properly.

Additionally, personal finance greatly influences our relationships and social connections. Money-related conflicts are one of the leading causes of stress within partnerships and families. We can cultivate open communication and collaboration by improving our money management abilities, which will result in healthier relationships and stronger support systems.

Furthermore, understanding personal finance empowers individuals to make informed decisions about their long-term financial goals, such as retirement savings or purchasing a home.

1.4 Overcoming Fears and Gaining Confidence in Managing Money

Managing finances can often be daunting, and many people may feel overwhelmed or anxious about their personal finances. However, it's essential to recognize that everyone can over-come these fears and gain confidence in managing money.

One common fear is the fear of making mistakes or poor financial decisions. This fear can hold individuals from taking action or making necessary changes to improve their financial situation. However, it's important to understand that making mistakes is a natural learning process. By embracing these mis-takes as opportunities for growth and learning, you can build resilience and develop a stronger understanding of personal finance.

Another fear that many people face is the fear of confronting their financial reality. It can be uncomfortable to face the truth about one's financial situation, especially if it involves debt or financial struggles. However, avoiding or ignoring these issues will only exacerbate the problem in the long run. By confronting your financial reality head-on, you can identify areas for improvement and develop a plan to overcome any challenges.

Addressing any limiting beliefs or negative mindsets sur-rounding money is also important. Many people have been conditioned to believe certain myths or misconceptions about personal finance, such as "money is evil" or "rich people are greedy." These beliefs can create a negative association with money and hinder one's ability to manage it effectively. By challenging these beliefs and adopting a more positive mindset towards money, you can shift your perspective and develop a healthier relationship with your finances.

Building confidence in managing money requires education and knowledge. By seeking out resources such as books, podcasts, or online courses, you can expand your financial literacy and better understand personal finance concepts. Taking the time to educate yourself will help alleviate fears and empower you to make informed decisions about your money.

Lastly, surrounding yourself with a supportive community or seeking professional guidance can also build confidence in managing money. Connecting with others who have similar goals or aspirations can provide a sense of accountability and motivation. Additionally, working with a financial advisor or coach can offer personalized guidance and expertise tailored to your specific needs and circumstances.

1.5 Taking The First Steps towards Financial Independence

Now that you understand the importance of personal finance, it's time to take the first steps toward achieving financial independence.

The road to financial independence begins with education and understanding. Educating yourself about the basic principles of personal finance, such as budgeting, saving, debt management, and investing, is essential. You'll be equipped with the tools and strategies necessary to make informed financial decisions by gaining knowledge in these areas.

One of the initial steps towards financial independence is assessing your current financial situation. Take the time to evaluate your income, expenses, assets, and liabilities. This self-assessment will give you a clear picture of where you stand financially and help you identify areas for improvement. It will also enable you to set realistic goals and develop a plan to achieve them.

As you embark on your journey towards financial independence, it's essential to establish a strong foundation by creating a budget. A budget will serve as your roadmap for managing your money wisely. It will help you track your income and expenses, prioritize your spending, and ensure you live within your means. By following a budget, you can avoid overspending, reduce unnecessary costs, and allocate funds toward savings and investments.

Another crucial step towards financial independence is developing healthy spending habits. It's essential to differentiate between wants and needs and make mindful purchase decisions. Avoiding impulsive buying behavior and curbing unnecessary expenses will allow you to save more effectively and make progress toward your financial goals.

Additionally, taking control of your debt is vital for financial independence. Develop a debt repayment plan based on your current financial situation and prioritize paying off high-interest debts first. Implement debt consolidation or negotiation with creditors to simplify payments and reduce interest rates. As you work towards debt-free, maintain good credit by making timely payments and avoiding excessive borrowing.

Finally, don't underestimate the power of building an emergency fund. Life is full of unexpected events, and having a financial cushion will provide stability and peace of mind. Start by setting aside a small amount from each paycheck until you have accumulated at least three to six months' living expenses. This fund will protect you from unforeseen circumstances and prevent you from relying on credit cards or loans during emergencies.

Taking the first steps toward financial independence requires commitment, discipline, and perseverance. It may not always be easy, but remember that every small action you take brings you closer to achieving your financial goals. Stay motivated, stay focused, and believe in yourself. Dedication and knowledge gained from this book give you the power to shape your financial future.

1.6 Wrapping It Up

In this chapter, we've explored the importance of personal finance in today's world and why it matters for your overall well-being. We debunked common misconceptions about personal finance and discussed overcoming fears and gaining confidence in managing your money. Understanding the impact of personal finance on your life is the first step towards creating a solid foundation for your financial journey. By gaining knowledge and developing the necessary skills, you'll be equipped to make informed decisions and take control of your financial future.

Remember, personal finance is not just about numbers and spreadsheets; it's about empowering yourself to live the life you desire. It's about achieving your dreams, whether owning a home, starting a business, or enjoying a comfortable retirement. Financial literacy is the key that opens doors to endless possibilities.

As we proceed further into this book, I encourage you to embrace this opportunity to transform your financial situation. Each chapter will provide valuable insights, practical strategies, and actionable steps to help you master money skills and achieve financial success.

Chapter 2 will explore the power of a financial mindset and discover how to align your values with your financial goals. Remember, you can shape your financial future, and with the proper knowledge and tools, you can create a path toward financial freedom.

Chapter 2: The Power of Financial Mindset

"Your mindset is the foundation upon which your financial success is built."

When it comes to financial success, it's all about that mindset game. Your mindset is like the architect of your financial empire. It's the blueprint, the foundation, the whole shebang. Think about it - you can have all the money-saving tips and investment tricks in the world, but if your mindset needs to be on point, it's like building a house on shaky ground.

So, picture this: Your mindset is the chief engineer, ensuring every decision is solid and every move is calculated. It's not just about dollars and cents; it's about approaching challenges, embracing opportunities, and navigating the financial roller-coaster.

In the previous chapter, we discussed the importance of personal finance and how it can positively impact every aspect of our lives. In Chapter 2, we will delve deeper into the power of the financial mindset and how it plays a crucial role in achieving our financial goals and priorities.

Financial success is not solely determined by how much money we earn or our investments. It begins with having the right mindset that aligns our values with our financial goals and empowers us to take control of our financial future.

This chapter will explore how our mindset influences our relationship with money, uncovering any limiting beliefs or misconceptions we may have. We will learn how to cultivate a positive mindset towards money and wealth, overcoming any barriers that may hold us back from achieving our full financial potential.

Furthermore, we will discuss the importance of setting SMART financial goals – specific, measurable, Achievable, relevant, and time-bound goals. By understanding the power of goal-setting, we can prioritize and develop an action plan to turn our aspirations into realities.

Throughout this chapter, I will share personal experiences and insights that have shaped my financial mindset and helped me overcome obstacles on my journey toward financial independence. I will also provide practical guidance and exercises to help you identify your values, align them with your financial goals, and develop a positive and resilient mindset to guide you toward long-term financial success.

By the end of this chapter, you will understand how your mindset influences your financial well-being and be equipped with the tools and knowledge to set meaningful financial goals based on your values and priorities.

2.1 Identifying Your Values and Aligning Them with Your Financial Goals

Understanding your financial goals and priorities begins with recognizing your values and how they relate to money. Your values are the fundamental beliefs and principles that guide your life and are crucial in shaping your financial decisions.

Take some time for self-reflection and identify what truly matters to you. Is it security, freedom, family, or personal growth? Understanding your values can align your financial goals with what you hold dear.

For example, if family is your top priority, your financial goals may include saving for your child's education or creating a stable future for your loved ones. On the other hand, if personal growth is essential, you might prioritize investing in education or experiences that expand your knowledge and skills.

Aligning your values with your financial goals creates a sense of purpose and motivation. It clarifies why you're working towards specific objectives and helps you stay committed during challenging times.

Once you have identified your values, examine how they align with your financial behaviors. Are you spending money in a way that reflects what you truly value? Or are there areas where your spending is not aligned with your priorities?

For instance, if you value health and well-being but frequently splurge on unhealthy snacks or gym memberships you don't use, it may be time to reassess your spending habits and reallocate funds towards activities that authentically support your values.

2.2 Cultivating a positive mindset towards money

It is essential to cultivate a positive mindset towards money. Our beliefs and attitudes about money profoundly impact our financial decisions and behaviors. By shifting our mindset from scarcity to abundance, we can open ourselves up to new opportunities and possibilities for financial growth.

One of the first steps in cultivating a positive mindset towards money is to recognize and challenge our limiting beliefs about wealth. Many of us grow up with certain beliefs about money that may not serve us in our journey toward financial independence. These beliefs may include thoughts such as "money is evil" or "rich people are greedy." By questioning these beliefs and reframing them in a more positive light, we can begin to embrace the idea that money is simply a tool that can help us achieve our goals and positively impact the world.

Another aspect of cultivating a positive mindset towards money is developing gratitude for what we already have. It's easy to focus on what we lack or wish we had, but by shifting our perspective to gratitude, we can attract more abundance into our lives. Take a moment each day to reflect on what you are grateful for a stable job, a supportive network of friends and family, or even just the basic necessities like food and shelter. By expressing gratitude for what you already have, you create space for more good things to come your way.

Visualization is another powerful tool for cultivating a positive mindset towards money. Take time each day to visualize your financial goals as if they have already been achieved. Picture yourself living in your dream home, driving your dream car, or taking that dream vacation. Visualizing your goals in vivid detail sends a powerful message to your subconscious mind that these goals are achievable and within reach.

Lastly, surrounding yourself with positive influences can significantly impact your financial mindset. Seek mentors or role models who have achieved the financial success you desire. Read books, listen to podcasts, or attend personal finance and wealth creation seminars. By immersing yourself in a positive environment, you will be motivated and inspired to take action towards achieving your own financial goals.

2.3 Recognizing and overcoming limiting beliefs about wealth

To truly master personal finance and achieve financial success, we must recognize and overcome any limiting beliefs we may have about wealth. These beliefs, often ingrained in us from childhood or influenced by societal norms, can hinder our ability to manage money wisely and make sound financial decisions.

One common limiting belief is that wealth is reserved for a select few or that it is immoral or unethical to accumulate wealth. This belief can stem from cultural or societal conditioning that emphasizes the virtues of modesty and selflessness. However, it is essential to reframe this belief and understand that when acquired ethically, wealth can be a powerful tool for personal growth and a positive impact on society.

Another limiting belief is that money is scarce and will never be enough to meet our needs and desires. This scarcity mindset can lead to a fear of spending or investing money, ultimately inhibiting our ability to grow financially. By shifting our mindset to one of abundance, we can cultivate a sense of confidence and trust in our ability to attract and manage wealth.

Furthermore, many individuals struggle with guilt or shame associated with money. This could be due to past financial mistakes or believing they do not deserve financial success. Acknowledging these emotions and working on developing a healthy relationship with money, free from guilt or shame, is important.

It is crucial to engage in self-reflection and challenge the assumptions we hold about wealth. This may involve seeking the guidance of a financial coach or therapist who can help us identify and reframe our beliefs. Additionally, surrounding ourselves with like-minded individuals on a similar journey toward financial empowerment can provide invaluable support and encouragement.

It is also helpful to seek out inspiring stories of individuals who have overcome similar limiting beliefs and achieved financial success. These stories remind us that anyone can create a prosperous future by adopting a growth mindset and taking consistent action toward their financial goals.

2.4 Setting SMART financial goals

It is crucial to set clear and achievable goals. However, not all goals are created equal. That is when the SMART goal framework stands out.

SMART stands for Specific, Measurable, Achievable, Relevant, and Time-bound. By following this framework, you can create well-defined, trackable, and realistically attainable goals within a specific timeframe. Let's break down each component of a **SMART** goal.

Specific: When setting financial goals, be as specific as possible. Instead of saying, "I want to save money," specify how much you want to save and for what purpose. For example, "I want to save $10,000 within the next two years for a down payment on a house."

Measurable: A goal should have a quantifiable measure of progress. This allows you to track your progress and stay motivated along the way. Using the previous example, you can measure your progress by setting monthly or quarterly savings targets.

Achievable: It is important to set goals that are realistically attainable based on your current financial situation. While it is good to aim high, setting unattainable goals can lead to frustration and demotivation. Consider your income, expenses, and timeline when determining if a goal is achievable.

Relevant: Your goal should align with your overall financial priorities and values. Ask yourself if achieving this goal will bring you closer to financial stability, security, or any other important aspect of your financial well-being.

Time-bound: Setting a deadline for your goal adds a sense of urgency and helps you stay focused. Without a timeframe, it becomes easy to procrastinate or lose motivation. Assign a specific deadline to your goal, such as "I will save $10,000 within the next two years."

It is important to note that setting SMART goals is not a one-time exercise. As your circumstances change and you achieve specific goals, you must revisit and adjust your goals accordingly. Regularly reviewing and updating your goals ensures that they remain relevant and motivating.

2.5 Prioritizing financial goals and developing an action plan

Once you have set your financial goals, the next step is to prioritize them and develop a clear action plan. You can focus your efforts and resources on what matters most to you by prioritizing your goals. This will help you stay motivated and progress towards achieving your desired financial outcomes.

To prioritize your goals effectively, start by considering the urgency and importance of each goal. Urgent goals require immediate attention, such as paying off high-interest debt or building an emergency fund. Important goals align with your long-term financial well-being, such as retirement savings or purchasing a home.

Consider each goal's impact on your overall financial situation and personal fulfillment. Some goals may have a more significant positive impact, while others may align more with your values and aspirations. Take the time to reflect on what truly matters to you and what will contribute to your long-term happiness and security.

Once you have determined the priority of each goal, it's time to develop an action plan. Break down each goal into smaller, manageable steps to achieve its achievement. For example, one of your goals is to save for a down payment on a house. In that case, you can create a plan that includes saving a certain amount each month, researching mortgage options, and attending first-time homebuyer workshops.

Write down your action plan and set target dates for completing each step. This will help you stay organized and accountable for your goals. Remember to be realistic about the time and resources required for each step. It's okay if your action plan evolves over time – flexibility is key in personal finance.

Keep in mind that prioritizing goals is about paying attention to other goals. It means allocating your time, energy, and money wisely so that you can make meaningful progress toward what matters most to you. You can constantly reassess and adjust your priorities as you achieve one goal.

Incorporate regular check-ins and evaluations into your action plan to ensure that you are making progress toward your financial goals. Celebrate small wins along the way to keep yourself motivated and encouraged. Remember, personal

23

finance is a journey, and achieving financial success is not just about reaching the destination but also enjoying the process.

2.6 The Role of Discipline, Consistency, and Resilience in Achieving Financial Success

To truly master money skills and achieve financial success, it is essential to cultivate discipline, consistency, and resilience. These qualities are the foundation for building healthy financial habits and overcoming obstacles.

Discipline plays a crucial role in managing your finances effectively. It involves making intentional choices that align with your long-term goals, even when faced with temptations or immediate gratification. For example, discipline may mean resisting the urge to make impulsive purchases or sticking to your budget even when tempting sales or promotions exist. You can avoid unnecessary debt and control your financial decisions by exercising discipline.

Consistency is equally important in financial management. This involves developing a routine and sticking to it, whether tracking your expenses regularly, setting aside a portion of your income for monthly savings, or paying bills on time. Consistency helps establish healthy financial habits that become second nature over time. You build a solid foundation for long-term financial growth and stability by consistently practicing good money habits.

However, it's important to acknowledge that setbacks and challenges are inevitable on the path to financial success. This is where resilience comes into play. Resilience is the ability to bounce back from setbacks, learn from failures, and stay motivated despite adversity. It's normal to experience financial setbacks such as unexpected expenses or market downturns. How you respond and adapt ultimately determines your success. Resilience enables you to navigate challenges, adjust your plans, and focus on your long-term goals.

Developing discipline, consistency, and resilience requires self-awareness and self-reflection. Take the time to evaluate your strengths and weaknesses when managing money. Identify areas where you need more discipline or consistency and develop strategies to overcome obstacles. Surround yourself with a supportive network of family or friends who share similar financial goals and can provide accountability and encouragement along the way.

2.7 Wrapping It Up

In this chapter, we have explored the power of a financial mindset and how it impacts our ability to achieve our financial goals. By understanding our values and aligning them with our financial aspirations, we can create a solid foundation for success.

We have also delved into the importance of cultivating a positive mindset towards money and overcoming limiting beliefs about wealth. By adopting a growth mindset and embracing abundance, we open ourselves to new opportunities and possibilities for financial growth.

Setting SMART financial goals is another crucial aspect we discussed in this chapter. By making our goals specific, measurable, attainable, relevant, and time-bound, we increase our chances of success and keep ourselves focused on what truly matters.

Moreover, we have emphasized the role of discipline, consistency, and resilience in achieving financial success. Building good habits and maintaining motivation throughout our journey are vital factors that contribute to long-term financial well-being.

Now that you have a deeper understanding of the power of a financial mindset, please take some time to reflect on your own mindset and beliefs about money. Consider how they may influence your financial situation and identify any areas you need to adjust.

In the next chapter, we will dive into the practical aspect of personal finance – creating a budget. This essential tool will be the foundation for managing money wisely and achieving financial goals.

Chapter 3: Creating a Budget

"Budgeting is not about limiting your financial freedom; it's about empowering yourself to make intentional choices that align with your financial goals."

Budgeting gets a bad rap sometimes. People think it's all about restriction and saying 'no' to everything fun. But let me tell you, it's the total opposite. Budgeting is like your financial GPS, guiding you toward your goals on your bucket list.

In today's fast-paced and ever-changing world, taking control of your personal finances is more important than ever. Establishing a solid foundation for financial success is essential, starting with creating a budget. A budget serves as a roadmap to guide your financial decisions, ensuring that you control your money rather than letting it control you.

In Chapter 3, we will delve into the world of budgeting, providing you with the necessary tools and knowledge to create a budget that works for you. By understanding the purpose and benefits of budgeting, identifying different budgeting methods, and setting aside savings, you will be well-equipped to manage your money wisely.

Throughout this chapter, we will explore various strategies to ensure budgeting becomes integral to your financial journey. By the end of this chapter, you will have the confidence and skills to develop a realistic spending plan and take charge of your financial future.

3.1 The Purpose and Benefits of Budgeting

Budgeting is a fundamental tool for achieving financial success. It allows individuals to gain control of their finances, make informed decisions, and prioritize their spending. By creating a budget, you can allocate your income towards essential needs, savings, and debt repayment while ensuring you have enough money for discretionary expenses.

One of the primary purposes of budgeting is to provide a clear picture of your financial situation. It helps you understand where your money is coming from and where it is going. This awareness allows you to identify areas where you may need to spend more money or allocate more funds. With this knowledge, you can adjust and take proactive steps to improve your financial health.

Budgeting also plays a crucial role in reducing financial stress. When you have a budget in place, you no longer have to worry about whether you will have enough money to cover your expenses or unexpected emergencies. Instead, you can approach your finances with confidence and peace of mind, knowing you have a plan.

In addition, budgeting helps you set financial goals and work towards achieving them. Whether saving for a down payment on a house, paying off debt, or planning for retirement, a budget provides the framework for allocating funds toward these goals. By tracking your progress through regular budget reviews, you can stay motivated and make any necessary adjustments along the way.

Moreover, budgeting promotes financial responsibility and discipline. It encourages individuals to consider their spending choices carefully and prioritize their needs over wants. By being mindful of how you allocate your money, you can avoid impulse purchases and unnecessary expenses that may derail your financial goals.

Lastly, budgeting enables individuals to anticipate and plan for future expenses. By allocating funds towards savings or sinking funds, you can be prepared for predictable costs such as car repairs, medical bills, or vacations. This proactive approach prevents you from relying on credit or incurring debt when these expenses arise unexpectedly.

3.2 Different Budgeting Methods and Finding The One that Works for You

A budget serves as the foundation of your financial planning. It allows you to allocate your income wisely, ensuring you have enough funds for your needs, wants, and future goals. Budgeting methods can vary depending on individual prefer- ences, financial goals, and lifestyle. Let's take a look at some commonly used methods.

Traditional Budgeting: This method involves tracking and categorizing every expense manually. You maintain a record of your income, fixed expenses such as rent or mortgage payments, utilities, and variable expenses like groceries, dining out, entertainment, etc. This approach requires discipline and meticulous tracking but provides a comprehensive overview of your spending habits.

Percentage-Based Budgeting: With this method, you allocate a percentage of your income to different expense categories. For example, you might designate 50% for necessities (rent/mortgage, utilities, groceries), 30% for wants (dining out, entertainment), and 20% for savings or debt repayment. This method ensures you prioritize important expenses while leaving room for discretionary spending.

Zero-Based Budgeting: Zero-based budgeting requires assigning every dollar of your income to an expense category or savings goal. You start with zero at the beginning of each month and give each dollar a job, whether paying bills, saving for emergencies, or contributing to long-term goals. This method encourages a mindful allocation of resources and helps eliminate wasteful spending.

Envelope System: The envelope system divides your cash into envelopes labeled with different expense categories. Each envelope represents a specific expenditure, such as groceries, transportation, or entertainment. You take cash from the corresponding envelope as you spend money in each category. Once an envelope is empty, you know you've reached the limit for that category.

Digital Budgeting Apps: In today's digital age, numerous budgeting apps are available that simplify the process of tracking and managing finances. These apps sync with your bank accounts, credit cards, and other financial institutions to automatically categorize expenses and provide insights into your spending habits.

Finding the proper budgeting method for yourself requires some trial and error. Take the time to evaluate your financial goals, preferences, and personal circumstances. Consider factors such as your income stability, desired level of organization, and technological comfort. Experiment with different methods until you find one that aligns with your needs and effectively helps you achieve your financial objectives.

3.3 Identifying and Prioritizing Financial Needs vs. Wants

When it comes to managing your finances, one of the most crucial skills you need to develop is distinguishing between your financial needs and wants. Understanding the differences between these two categories will help you create a budget that aligns with your goals and values.

Financial needs are the essential expenses required for your basic survival and well-being. These include necessities such as food, shelter, clothing, transportation, and healthcare. Needs are non-negotiable expenses that you must prioritize in your budget to ensure your fundamental needs are met.

On the other hand, financial wants are expenditures beyond

our basic needs that provide enjoyment or convenience but are not essential for survival. These include dining out at restaurants, entertainment expenses, vacations, and luxury goods. While wants can add value to our lives, they should be carefully evaluated and prioritized within the constraints of our budget.

To identify your financial needs, list all your monthly fixed expenses, such as rent or mortgage payments, utility bills, insurance premiums, and loan repayments. These are recurring obligations that must be fulfilled to maintain a stable lifestyle.

Next, consider your variable expenses, which can vary monthly. These may include groceries, transportation costs, and other miscellaneous expenses. By tracking your spending for a few months, you can calculate an average for each category and estimate how much you typically spend on these variable expenses.

Once you have identified your financial needs, it's important to prioritize them within your budget. Allocate a portion of your income towards your essential expenses before considering any discretionary spending. By ensuring that your needs are covered before indulging in wants, you can establish a solid foundation for financial stability.

Now, let's discuss wants. While it's tempting to fulfill all our desires immediately, it's important to exercise restraint and carefully evaluate each wants about our financial goals. Ask yourself questions like:

How does this "want" align with my values and long-term finan-cial goals?

Can I afford this "want" without jeopardizing my financial needs?

Will this "want" bring me long-lasting satisfaction, or is it just a temporary pleasure?

Reflecting on these questions will help you make more in-formed choices when fulfilling your wants. Remember that delaying gratification today can lead to greater financial free-dom and security tomorrow.

3.4 Budgeting for Irregular Expenses

Many people often overlook the importance of accounting for irregular expenses when it comes to budgeting. These are expenses that don't occur on a monthly basis or have fluctuating amounts, making them tricky to anticipate and plan for. However, failing to include these expenses in your budget can lead to financial stress and derail your overall financial goals.

Irregular expenses can include annual subscriptions, quarterly insurance payments, vehicle repairs, home maintenance costs, medical bills, and even holiday or birthday gifts. These ex-penses may not occur every month, but they can still signifi-cantly impact your budget when they do arise.

To effectively budget for irregular expenses, start by identify-ing the common irregular expenses you incur throughout the year. Please take note of their average costs and the frequency at which they occur. This will help you estimate how much to allocate for these monthly expenses.

One strategy is to create a separate savings account specifically for irregular expenses. Set aside a portion of your income each month into this account to build up a cushion for when these irregular expenses arise. By doing so, you won't have to scramble to find the money or rely on credit when the time comes.

Another approach is to break down the cost of irregular expenses into smaller monthly amounts. For example, if your car requires an annual maintenance check that costs $600, you can set aside $50 monthly. This allows you to spread the financial impact of irregular expenses and ensure you have enough funds when the time comes.

Remember to review and adjust your budget regularly to accommodate any changes in your irregular expenses. As the year goes on, new expenses may emerge, or existing ones may increase or decrease in cost. By staying vigilant and proactive, you can ensure that your budget remains aligned with your actual financial needs.

Furthermore, it's essential to prioritize these irregular expenses based on their importance and urgency. Some irregular expenses may be more critical than others and require immediate attention. You can address the most pressing irregular expenses by allocating funds accordingly without compromising your overall financial stability.

3.5 Reviewing and Adjusting the Budget Regularly for Optimal Results

Once you have created a budget, it is crucial to review and adjust it regularly to ensure that it remains effective in helping you achieve your financial goals. Life is constantly changing, and your budget should adapt accordingly. Periodically reviewing and adjusting your budget can optimize your financial planning and make necessary changes to stay on track.

Reviewing your budget allows you to assess if your spending aligns with your financial priorities and goals. It provides an opportunity to evaluate whether you are allocating your resources wisely and making progress toward your desired financial outcomes. By reviewing your budget, you can identify areas where you may be overspending or where adjustments can be made to maximize savings.

During the review process, carefully analyze each category of expenses. Look for patterns or trends that may have emerged since the last review. Are there any areas where you consistently overspend? Are there any unexpected expenses that have come up? Understanding these patterns will help you make informed decisions about adjustments that need to be made.

Adjusting your budget based on the review findings is essential for maintaining financial stability and achieving long-term goals. This may involve reallocating funds between categories, cutting back on certain expenses, or finding ways to increase your income. The goal is to ensure that your budget reflects your current financial situation and aligns with your evolving priorities.

3.6 Wrapping It Up

In this chapter, we explored the importance of creating a budget as the foundation for achieving financial success. By now, you should understand that a budget is not just about restricting your spending; it is a powerful tool that lets you control your money and prioritize your financial goals.

We discussed various budgeting methods and encouraged you to find the one that works best for you. Whether it's the traditional envelope system or using budgeting apps, the key is to choose a method that aligns with your preferences and helps you stay organized.

Creating a realistic spending plan is an essential step in budgeting. It involves setting aside savings and ensuring that your expenses align with your income. Remember, a budget should be flexible and adaptable, allowing room for unexpected expenses or changes in financial circumstances.

Regularly reviewing and adjusting your budget is necessary to ensure that it continues to meet your needs and goals. As your financial situation evolves, so should your budget. By regularly monitoring your spending habits and making necessary adjustments, you can stay on track toward achieving financial success.

With the information in this chapter, you now have the knowledge and tools to create an adequate budget to help you manage your money wisely. In the next chapter, we will delve into the importance of tracking income and expenses and how gaining control over your finances can significantly impact your overall financial well-being.

Chapter 4: Tracking Income and Expenses

"Money isn't the most important thing in life, but it's reasonably close to oxygen on the 'gotta have it' scale." - Zig Ziglar

This quote hit the nail on the head with that one. Money might not be the be-all and end-all, but let's be honest – it's pretty darn essential, like oxygen for our financial survival.

I mean, think about it. You can't pay the bills with good vibes and positive thoughts. Money gives you the freedom to breathe and live on your terms. It's not about worshiping the almighty dollar; it's about recognizing that financial stability opens up a world of possibilities.

Picture this: Money is the oxygen mask in the financial turbulence of life. When you have it, you can breathe easy and focus on the things that truly matter – family, experiences, and personal growth. It's not just about accumulating wealth for its own sake; it's about creating a buffer, a safety net, ensuring you're not gasping for air when unexpected challenges hit.

In today's fast-paced world, keeping track of our income

and expenses can feel daunting. However, understanding where our money comes from and where it goes is crucial for gaining control of our finances. Tracking our income and expenses allows us to make informed decisions, identify areas of overspending or inefficiency, and ultimately achieve our financial goals.

In this chapter, we will explore the various strategies and techniques to effectively track our income and expenses. We will learn how to establish a reliable system, organize financial documents, and utilize technology to streamline the process. Additionally, we will delve into the importance of analyzing spending patterns and identifying areas of improvement.

By implementing the practices discussed in this chapter, you will develop the skills necessary to manage your finances. You will gain greater awareness of your financial habits and be able to make conscious choices about how you allocate your resources. Tracking your income and expenses will pave the way toward financial stability and success.

4.1 Establishing a System for Tracking Income and Expenses

Tracking income and expenses is essential for controlling your finances and understanding where your money goes. By establishing a system for tracking your income and expenses, you can clearly understand your financial situation and make informed decisions about your spending habits.

One way to track your income is by keeping a record of all

the money you make. This includes not only your salary or wages but also any additional sources of income, such as rental properties, side gigs, or investment dividends. By documenting all your sources of income, you can accurately assess your total earnings and plan accordingly.

On the other hand, tracking expenses involves recording every dollar you spend. This includes necessary expenses like rent, utilities, groceries, and discretionary spending on entertainment, dining out, or shopping. By diligently keeping track of all your expenses, you can identify any areas of overspending and make adjustments to stay within your budget.

You can use various tools and methods to establish an effective system for tracking income and expenses. One common approach is to use a spreadsheet or budgeting software that allows you to input and categorize each transaction. This way, you can quickly see how much money is coming in and going out, and you can analyze your spending patterns over time.

Another option is to utilize mobile apps designed explicitly for expense tracking. These apps often sync with your bank accounts and credit cards, automatically categorizing transactions for you. They can provide real-time updates on your spending habits and help you stay accountable to your financial goals.

Regardless of the method you choose, consistency is critical. Make it a habit to record every transaction promptly, ensuring no expense slips through the cracks. Review your income and expenses regularly to track your progress toward financial goals and identify any areas that require adjustment.

4.2 Organizing Financial Documents Effectively

One of the critical aspects of gaining control over your finances is organizing your financial documents effectively. Keeping track of important papers, receipts, and statements allows you to clearly understand your income and expenses, making it easier to manage your money wisely.

It's always helpful to create a filing system that works for you. Consider using categories such as income, bills, debt, savings, investments, insurance, and taxes. Within each category, you can further organize documents by date or type. For example, you can have subcategories for utilities, rent/mortgage, and subscriptions within the bills category.

It's essential to keep physical and digital copies of your financial documents. Physical copies provide a tangible backup in case of technological failures or emergencies. Digital copies are convenient for easy access and organization. Consider investing in a scanner or a mobile scanning app to convert physical documents into digital formats.

When it comes to storing physical copies, use a secure and fireproof filing cabinet or box. Label each folder clearly to avoid confusion when retrieving specific documents. Create a dedicated folder on your computer or cloud storage service for digital copies. Make sure to password-protect sensitive financial information for added security.

As you receive financial documents such as pay stubs, bank statements, and bills, be proactive in organizing them right away. Please resist the temptation to leave them lying around or stacking up on your desk. Please take a few minutes each week to file new documents in their respective categories. This small effort will save you time and frustration in the long run.

In addition to organizing your financial documents, consider creating a master spreadsheet or using personal finance software to digitally track your income and expenses. This lets you easily track and categorize transactions, analyze spending patterns, and generate detailed reports for better financial insights.

4.3 Utilizing Technology and Digital Tools for Expense Tracking

Technology has become an integral part of our daily lives in today's fast-paced world. It has also revolutionized the way we manage our finances. With the help of various digital tools and mobile applications, tracking your income and expenses has never been easier.

Gone are the days of manually recording every transaction in a ledger or spreadsheet. Now, you can download budgeting apps or use online platforms to automatically track your expenses and analyze your spending patterns. These tools save time and provide valuable insights into your financial habits.

Some apps allow you to link your bank accounts, credit cards, and other financial accounts in one place. It automatically categorizes your transactions, providing you with an overview of where your money is going. You can set budgets for different categories, receive alerts for bill payments, and even track your credit score.

Some apps focus on helping you stay within your budget. It tracks your income and expenses and shows how much money you have left to spend after accounting for bills, savings, and goals. It also provides tips on how to save more efficiently and avoid unnecessary expenses.

For those who prefer manual tracking, spreadsheets like Google Sheets or Microsoft Excel offer customizable templates to record your income and expenses. You can create separate sheets for different categories, such as housing, transportation, groceries, and entertainment. You can easily calculate your total expenses and compare them to your budget by inputting your transactions regularly.

Furthermore, online banking platforms provide detailed transaction histories that you can access anytime. By logging into your bank account's website or mobile app, you can review past purchases and filter them by date or category. Some banks even offer personalized spending reports to help you analyze your financial behavior over time.

4.4 Categorizing Expenses

Tracking your income and expenses is essential to gaining control over your finances. But it's not enough to simply record your expenses. To truly understand where your money is going and how you can improve, you need to categorize your expenses and identify areas for potential savings.

Categorizing expenses allows you to see patterns and trends in your spending habits. It helps you visualize how much you are spending on different aspects of your life, such as housing, transportation, food, entertainment, and so on. This breakdown provides valuable insights into where your money is being allocated and whether it aligns with your financial goals.

To start categorizing your expenses, you can create a spreadsheet or use budgeting apps that allow you to assign each expense to a specific category. The categories can be as broad or as detailed as you prefer, depending on the level of granularity you want in analyzing your expenses.

4.5 Analyzing Spending Patterns and Identifying Areas of Overspending or Inefficiency

One of the critical steps towards mastering personal finance is gaining a clear understanding of your spending patterns. By analyzing your expenses, you can identify areas where you may be overspending or inefficient with your money. This knowledge will allow you to make informed decisions and take necessary actions to improve your financial situation.

Now that you have categorized your expenses, take a closer look at each category to identify any patterns or trends. Are there any categories where you consistently spend more than you intended? Are there any categories where you could potentially cut back or find more cost-effective alternatives?

For example, if you notice that a large portion of your budget is allocated to dining out, consider cooking meals at home more often. Not only will this save you money, but it can also be healthier and more enjoyable as you explore new recipes and culinary skills.

Similarly, if you spend a significant amount on entertainment or subscriptions, assess whether you truly value and utilize all the services you are paying for. Canceling unnecessary subscriptions or finding more affordable alternatives can free up funds that can be redirected toward other financial goals.

Another aspect to consider when analyzing spending patterns is identifying any inefficiencies in your budget. Are there any recurring expenses that could be negotiated or minimized? For example, shopping around for better insurance rates or refinancing high-interest debt can help save money in the long run.

Additionally, be mindful of habits or behaviors that contribute to overspending. Are there specific triggers or emotional states that lead you to spend impulsively? By recognizing these patterns, you can develop strategies to curb impulsive buying behavior and ensure that your purchases align with your values and long-term financial goals.

Analyzing your spending patterns is an ongoing process. Regularly review your budget and track changes over time to see if adjustments need to be made. As you become more aware of your spending habits, you'll gain greater control over your finances and be able to make more intentional decisions about how you allocate your resources.

4.6 Strategies for Reducing Expenses without Compromising Quality of Life

To achieve financial stability and reach your savings goals, you should always find ways to reduce expenses without sacrificing the quality of your life.

One of the first steps in reducing expenses is to closely examine your spending patterns. Analyze your expenses over the past few months and identify areas where you can make some adjustments. We talked about this in the last section.

Another strategy for reducing expenses is to become a savvy shopper. Take the time to compare prices and look for deals before making a purchase. Use coupons, shop during sales, and take advantage of rewards programs to get the best value for your money. When buying groceries, consider planning meals in advance and creating a shopping list to avoid impulse purchases and minimize food waste.

Cutting back on discretionary spending is another effective way to reduce expenses. Take a critical look at your lifestyle and identify areas where you can make some adjustments. For example, instead of eating out at restaurants multiple times a week, try cooking at home more often. Consider packing your own lunch for work instead of buying it every day. Look for free or low-cost entertainment options such as local community events or outdoor activities.

It's also important to prioritize your needs over wants when it comes to making financial decisions. Before making a purchase, ask yourself if it is something you truly need or if it is simply something you want at the moment. By focusing on needs rather than wants, you can avoid unnecessary expenses and redirect your money towards more meaningful goals, such as saving for a vacation or building an emergency fund.

Furthermore, consider negotiating with service providers to lower your bills. Many companies are willing to negotiate with customers, especially if they have been loyal or face financial difficulties. Contact your cable or internet provider, insurance company, or cell phone carrier to see if they can offer you a better rate or discount. It doesn't hurt to ask; the potential savings can add up over time.

Lastly, adopting frugal habits can significantly reduce expenses in the long run. Look for ways to save money on everyday items such as energy-efficient appliances, LED light bulbs, and reusable products. Embrace DIY projects and learn new skills that can help you save money by doing things yourself instead of hiring professionals. Explore thrift stores and second-hand markets for affordable clothing and household items.

4.7 Developing Habits for Mindful Spending and Responsible Consumption

One of the key aspects of mindful spending is being aware of our values and aligning our financial decisions with them. This means considering the impact of our purchases on ourselves, others, and the environment. It involves evaluating whether a particular item or experience truly aligns with our values and brings us lasting fulfillment.

To cultivate mindful spending habits, you should identify the triggers and underlying causes of impulsive buying behavior. Often, impulse purchases stem from emotional or psychological factors such as stress, boredom, or a desire for instant gratification. By recognizing these triggers, we can develop strategies to curb impulsive buying and make more intentional choices.

Creating a realistic spending plan that reflects our values is another crucial step in practicing mindful spending. This plan should prioritize necessities over wants, ensuring we allocate our resources wisely. By evaluating purchases based on their value and long-term impact, we can avoid unnecessary expenses and focus on what truly matters to us.

To create a spending plan, start by categorizing your expenses into different categories, such as housing, transportation, food, utilities, entertainment, and savings. This will give you a clear picture of where your money is going and allow you to identify areas where you can cut back or make adjustments.

When setting your spending limits for each category, it's important to be realistic and take into account your income and financial obligations. Avoid setting unrealistic goals that will only lead to frustration and failure. Instead, focus on balancing your wants and needs while allowing room for savings and unexpected expenses.

Mindful spending also involves building resilience against persuasive marketing tactics. Advertisements often create a sense of urgency or influence our emotions to drive impulse buying. By understanding these tactics and questioning their true value, we can resist the pressure to spend impulsively and make more informed decisions.

In addition to creating a spending plan, regularly reviewing and adjusting your budget is crucial. Financial circumstances change over time, so it's important to adapt your budget accordingly. Review your spending habits periodically and identify areas where you can cut back or reallocate funds towards more meaningful goals.

4.8 Wrapping It Up

In this chapter, we explored the importance of tracking income and expenses to gain control of your finances. By establishing a system for tracking and organizing your financial documents, you can effectively monitor your spending patterns and identify areas of overspending or inefficiency.

We also discussed using technology and digital tools for expense tracking, which can significantly simplify the process and provide real-time insights into your financial habits. Analyzing these spending patterns allows you to make informed decisions about where you can cut expenses without compromising your quality of life.

By developing habits for mindful spending and responsible consumption, you can align your purchases with your values and prioritize necessities over wants. This promotes financial stability and contributes to a more sustainable lifestyle.

In addition, we highlighted the importance of building resilience against persuasive marketing tactics that often lead to impulsive buying behavior. By evaluating purchases based on value and long-term impact, you can make more informed decisions that are in line with your financial goals.

As we wrap up this chapter, I encourage you to apply the knowledge and strategies shared here to your financial situation. Remember, tracking income and expenses is not just about monitoring numbers on a spreadsheet; it is about gaining control over your financial well-being.

In the next chapter, we will delve into the topic of saving strategies and explore how you can build a solid financial cushion for future needs. By understanding the importance of saving and implementing effective strategies, you will be one step closer to mastering your money skills.

Chapter 5: Saving Strategies

"Saving money isn't about having less; it's about having more options."

Saving money – now, that's a game-changer. It's not about living with less; it's about opening up a world of possibilities. Picture it like a treasure chest of opportunities waiting to be unlocked.

When you save, you're not saying 'no' to things but saying 'yes' to options. It's like having a financial superpower, giving you the freedom to choose and to seize the opportunities that align with your dreams.

Imagine this: saving money is your ticket to a future full of options. Want to find a new career path? Build your dream home? Take that epic vacation? Saving is your passport to make those choices without financial stress.

In this chapter, we will explore various saving strategies to help you build a strong financial cushion, empowering you to take control of your financial future. Throughout this chapter, we will delve into the importance of saving and how it contributes to your overall financial well-being. We will identify short-term and long-term savings goals based on your needs and aspirations. Additionally, we will discuss different savings account options and investment vehicles that can maximize your potential returns.

Furthermore, we will discuss automating savings and ensuring consistency and discipline in your saving habits. By exploring strategies to cut expenses and increase your disposable income, we will help you create more room in your savings budget.

Moreover, we will touch on specialized savings such as emergency funds and retirement savings. These areas require tailored approaches to ensure that you are adequately prepared for unexpected financial challenges and to secure a comfortable retirement when the time comes.

By the end of this chapter, you will have gained invaluable insights into the importance of saving, developed effective strategies for building a robust financial cushion, and learned how to make your money work for you.

5.1 The Importance of Saving in Achieving Financial Stability and Security

Saving money is one of the fundamental aspects of personal finance that cannot be overstated. It serves as a key pillar in achieving financial stability and security. Saving allows you to build a strong financial cushion, providing you with peace of mind and the ability to handle unexpected expenses or emergencies effectively.

By saving regularly, you create a safety net that safeguards you from financial hardships. Whether it's an unexpected medical expense, car repair, or job loss, having savings allows you to navigate these challenges without falling into debt or experiencing extreme financial stress.

Moreover, saving money provides the opportunity for future investments and wealth accumulation. It empowers you to make strategic decisions about your financial future, such as buying a home, starting a business, or planning for retirement. Without savings, these aspirations remain distant dreams.

Additionally, saving helps break the cycle of living paycheck to paycheck. You can gradually reduce reliance on credit cards or loans to cover day-to-day expenses by consistently setting aside a portion of your income. This improves your overall financial health and gives you greater control over your money.

Furthermore, savings offer you greater flexibility and freedom in life choices. Whether pursuing further education, taking a sabbatical, or exploring new career opportunities, having a financial cushion gives you the confidence to take calculated risks and embrace new experiences.

5.2 Setting Savings Goals Based on Short-term and Long-term Needs

Setting savings goals is a crucial step in building a solid financial cushion. Without clear goals, staying motivated and focused on saving money can be challenging.

Short-term savings goals are those that you aim to achieve within a relatively short period, usually ranging from a few months to a year. These goals are typically more immediate and tangible, such as saving for a vacation, purchasing a new gadget, or building an emergency fund. Short-term goals help you stay disciplined and committed to saving regularly, as you can see the results quickly.

To set effective short-term savings goals, you should consider your current financial situation and prioritize accordingly. Start by identifying any immediate needs or wants that require financial resources. This could include upcoming events or expenses you know you will need to fund. Once you have recognized these priorities, assign a specific amount of money that you want to save for each goal. For example, if you are planning a vacation in six months and estimate that you will need $3,000, break it down into smaller monthly savings targets.

Long-term savings goals, on the other hand, are more focused on your future financial well-being. These goals can span several years or even decades, often encompass larger aspirations like buying a house, funding your children's education, or preparing for retirement. Long-term goals require patience, consistent saving habits, and careful planning.

When setting long-term savings goals, it is essential to take into account your desired lifestyle and the associated costs. Consider factors such as inflation rates, potential changes in income or expenses, and investment options that can help grow your savings over time. It may also be helpful to seek advice from professionals or utilize online tools to estimate the amount of money needed to reach specific long-term goals.

Remember that short-term and long-term savings goals should be realistic and attainable within your current financial circumstances. It is crucial not to overextend yourself financially or set unrealistic expectations. Break down larger goals into smaller milestones to track your progress and celebrate each accomplishment.

Setting clear savings goals based on your short-term and long-term needs empowers you with a roadmap toward financial security and success. These goals provide focus and motivation to consistently save money while ensuring you are prepared for immediate and future financial obligations. As you embark on your personal finance journey, remember that every dollar saved brings you closer to achieving your financial dreams.

5.3 Choosing the Right Savings Account or Investment Vehicle

Having a solid financial cushion is essential for long-term financial stability and security. One of the critical components of building this cushion is choosing the proper savings account or investment vehicle to help your money grow over time.

When it comes to saving, several options are available, each with its advantages and considerations. Let's take a look at some of the most common savings and investment vehicles to help you make an informed decision.

Traditional Savings Accounts: This is the most basic and widely used form of saving. Banks and credit unions offer traditional savings accounts, allowing you to deposit and withdraw funds easily. These accounts typically offer low interest rates but provide easy access to your money when needed. They work well for short-term goals or emergency funds that require liquidity.

Certificates of Deposit (CDs): CDs are time deposits earning higher interest rates than traditional savings accounts. With CDs, you agree to leave your money with a bank for a fixed period, ranging from a few months to several years. In return, you receive a higher interest rate. However, keep in mind that withdrawing your money before the CD matures usually incurs penalties.

Money Market Accounts (MMAs): MMAs are similar to traditional savings accounts but typically offer higher interest rates.

They combine features of both savings and checking accounts, providing limited check-writing capabilities and higher yields. MMAs usually require a higher minimum balance to open and maintain the account.

High-yield Savings Accounts: These online-based savings accounts often offer higher interest rates compared to traditional savings accounts or MMAs. They may have lower fees and minimum balance requirements while providing easy access to your funds through online and mobile banking platforms.

Retirement Accounts: Retirement accounts, such as Individual Retirement Accounts (IRAs) and 401(k)s, offer tax advantages while helping you save for retirement. Contributions to qualified retirement accounts may be tax-deductible or made with pre-tax dollars, allowing for potential long-term growth without immediate tax implications.

Investments: If you're willing to take on more risk for potentially higher returns, investing in stocks, bonds, mutual funds, or exchange-traded funds (ETFs) can be an option. It's important to understand that investing carries inherent risks, and past performance does not indicate future results. Consider seeking professional advice or conducting thorough research before venturing into investment opportunities.

When choosing the right savings account or investment vehicle, consider factors such as your financial goals, time horizon, risk tolerance, liquidity needs, and any associated fees or penalties. It's crucial to align your choice with your overall financial plan and diversify your savings across multiple vehicles for optimal risk management.

5.4 Automating Savings to Ensure Consistency and Discipline

One of the critical challenges in saving money is maintaining consistency and discipline. It's easy to get caught up in daily expenses and lose track of our savings goals. That's where automation comes in. By automating your savings, you can ensure that a portion of your income is consistently allocated towards your financial goals without any effort on your part.

Automating savings involves setting up recurring transfers from your checking account to your savings account or investment account. This can be done through online banking platforms or financial apps offering automatic savings features. Here are some benefits of automating your savings.

Consistency: Automating savings helps to establish a consistent savings habit. Setting up regular transfers eliminates the temptation to spend that money elsewhere. It becomes a routine, just like paying bills or other financial obligations.

Disciplined Saving: Automating savings removes the decision-making process from the equation. You don't have to constantly remind yourself to save; it happens automatically. This reduces the likelihood of succumbing to impulsive spending or neglecting your savings goals.

Peace of Mind: Knowing that your savings are being taken care of automatically gives you peace of mind. You don't have to worry about forgetting to save or falling behind on your goals. It allows you to focus on other aspects of your financial life without constantly worrying about saving enough.

Goal Tracking: When you automate your savings, tracking your progress toward your financial goals becomes easier. You can set specific targets for different purposes, such as an emergency fund, a down payment for a house, or retirement savings. Regularly monitoring your automated contributions helps you stay motivated and see how far you've come.

Time Efficiency: Automating savings saves you time and effort in managing your finances. Instead of manually transferring money each month, you can set it up once and let it run in the background. This frees up time for other important tasks or activities.

To get started with automating your savings, follow these steps.

1. Assess Your Financial Situation: Determine how much you can comfortably contribute towards savings each month. Look at your income, expenses, and financial goals to establish a realistic and achievable saving amount.

2. Set Up Recurring Transfers: Contact your bank or use financial apps offering automatic account transfers. They will guide you through the process of setting up recurring transfers based on your desired frequency (e.g., weekly, biweekly, monthly).

3. Allocate Funds Appropriately: Prioritize your savings goals and allocate funds accordingly. For example, if building an emergency fund is your top priority, direct a larger portion of your automated transfers toward this goal.

4. Review Regularly: Periodically review and adjust your automated saving plan as needed. Life circumstances change over time, and so may your financial goals or income levels. Make sure that your automated contributions align with your current needs and aspirations.

5.5 Strategies for Cutting Expenses and Increasing Disposable Income for Saving Purposes

In order to build a solid financial cushion and achieve your savings goals, finding ways to cut expenses and increase your disposable income is essential. While this may seem challenging at first, implementing some practical strategies can significantly affect your overall financial health.

Evaluate Your Monthly Expenses: Start by analyzing your monthly expenses and identifying areas where you can potentially cut back. Look for recurring expenses or subscriptions you no longer use or need. Canceling these unnecessary services can free up a significant amount of money that can be redirected towards savings.

Reduce Your Utility Bills: Energy costs can add up quickly, but there are several ways to minimize your utility bills without sacrificing comfort. Consider installing energy-efficient appliances and LED light bulbs. Also, be mindful of your water usage by fixing leaks and practicing water conservation techniques. Lowering your utility bills will save you money and contribute to a more sustainable lifestyle.

Plan Your Meals and Grocery Shopping: Eating out can be expensive, so developing the habit of preparing meals at home can lead to substantial savings. Create weekly meal plans and make a detailed shopping list to avoid impulse purchases at the grocery store. Take advantage of sales, discounts, and coupons to maximize your savings on food expenses while still enjoying delicious meals.

Slash Your Transportation Costs: Transportation expenses, including fuel/gas costs and vehicle maintenance, can take a significant portion of your budget. Consider carpooling or using public transportation whenever possible to reduce fuel costs. If you live in an area with good infrastructure for cycling, biking can be a cost-effective and eco-friendly alternative to driving. Additionally, consider downsizing to a more fuel-efficient vehicle or exploring car-sharing services to cut transportation expenses further.

Cut Down on Entertainment Expenses: Entertainment can drain your finances if not managed wisely. Look for free or low-cost activities in your community, such as local festivals, park outings, or hiking trails. Instead of going to the movie theater, consider renting movies or streaming services as a more affordable option. Additionally, explore free educational resources like libraries or online platforms for books and courses instead of purchasing them.

Negotiate Lower Utility Rates: Contact your service providers, such as cable, internet, and insurance companies, to negotiate better rates or find alternative options available in the market. Many companies offer promotions or loyalty discounts you may not know unless you inquire. Don't hesitate to shop around and compare prices for the best possible deals.

Minimize Impulse Buying: Impulse purchases can quickly add up and derail your budgeting efforts. Before making discretionary purchases, practice the "24-hour rule" by waiting 24 hours before buying anything non-essential. During this time, reflect on whether the purchase aligns with your financial goals and if it brings long-term value to your life.

5.6 Emergency Funds, Retirement Savings, and Other Types of Specialized Savings

In the journey towards financial independence, it is crucial to establish a strong foundation of savings that can provide a safety net during unexpected circumstances and ensure a comfortable retirement.

Building an Emergency Fund: The Path to Financial Resilience

Life is full of surprises, and not all of them are pleasant. Unexpected emergencies such as medical expenses, job loss, or car repairs can quickly derail your financial stability if you are unprepared. This is where an emergency fund comes into play, serving as a buffer against the unforeseen.

An emergency fund should ideally cover three to six months of living expenses. It should be easily accessible yet separate from your daily spending accounts to prevent any temptation to dip into it for non-emergency purposes.

Retirement Savings: Planning for a Secure Future

Retirement may seem distant, but planning for it early on is essential to enjoying the golden years of your life. We will discuss more in Chapter 12.

Other Types of Specialized Savings: Investing in Your Future

Beyond emergency funds and retirement savings, various other types of specialized savings accounts can help you achieve specific financial goals.

Below are some examples.

- Education Savings Accounts (ESA) or 529 Plans: Saving for future education expenses for yourself or your children.
- Health Savings Accounts (HSA) or Flexible Spending Accounts (FSA): Setting aside pre-tax dollars for healthcare expenses.
- Homeownership Savings Accounts: Accumulating funds for a down payment on a home or related expenses.
- Taxable Investment Accounts: Investing in stocks, bonds, or mutual funds outside of retirement accounts.

By understanding these specialized savings options and incorporating them into your overall financial plan, you can maximize the potential returns on your investments and work towards achieving various life goals.

5.7 Wrapping It Up

In this chapter, we explored the importance of saving in achieving financial stability and security. We discussed how setting savings goals based on short-term and long-term needs is crucial for building a strong financial cushion. By choosing the proper savings account or investment vehicle, individuals can make their money work harder for them.

Automating savings is an effective strategy to ensure consistency and discipline in saving. You can effortlessly build your savings by setting up automatic transfers from your paycheck or checking account to your savings account. We also discussed various strategies for cutting expenses and increasing disposable income for saving purposes.

In addition to general savings, we delved into specialized savings such as emergency funds and retirement savings. Emergency funds act as a safety net during unexpected financial emergencies, while retirement savings provide a nest egg for the golden years. We discussed the importance of contributing regularly to these specialized savings accounts to secure a financially comfortable future.

Building a strong financial cushion requires dedication, discipline, and perseverance. It may take time to reach your savings goals, but you can achieve financial peace of mind with consistent effort. By following the strategies outlined in this chapter, you will be well on your way to mastering the art of saving.

In the next chapter, we will explore another critical aspect of personal finance: debt management. We will discuss how to break free from the debt cycle by understanding different types of debt, creating a debt repayment plan, and maintaining good credit while repaying debt.

Chapter 6: Debt Management

"Your debt doesn't define you. Your actions to overcome it do."

Debt can often feel like a weight that holds us down, limiting our financial freedom and hindering our ability to achieve our goals. Whether it's student loans, credit card debt, or other forms of borrowing, being trapped in the debt cycle can be overwhelming and discouraging. However, it's essential to remember that you have the power to break free from this cycle and take control of your financial future.

In this chapter, we will explore various strategies and techniques for managing debt effectively. We will delve into understanding different types of debt and their implications, assessing your personal debt situation, and creating a customized debt repayment plan. Additionally, we will discuss debt consolidation options, negotiating with creditors for better terms, maintaining good credit while repaying debt, and developing long-term strategies to avoid future debt.

By equipping yourself with the knowledge and tools necessary to tackle your debts head-on, you can regain control over your finances and pave the way towards a brighter financial future.

6.1 Understanding Different Types of Debt and Their Implications

Debt is a common aspect of many people's financial lives, but it often carries a negative connotation. However, not all debt is inherently flawed. Understanding the different types of debt and their implications can help you make informed decisions and break free from the debt cycle.

One type of debt is called "good debt," which refers to borrowing money for investments that have the potential to increase in value or generate income over time. Examples of good debt may include student loans, mortgages, or business loans. These types of debts can be investments in your future, as they can improve your earning potential or provide a stable living situation.

On the other hand, there is also "bad debt," which typically includes high-interest consumer debts such as credit card debt or payday loans. Bad debt is often accrued for non-essential purchases or expenses that do not generate any long-term value. This type of debt can quickly become overwhelming and hinder your financial progress.

Understanding the implications of different types of debt is crucial for making smart financial decisions. Good debt can be an investment in your future. Still, it should be managed responsibly to ensure the benefits outweigh the costs. On the other hand, bad debt should be avoided whenever possible to prevent unnecessary financial stress and burdens.

When considering taking on debt, it's important to weigh the potential benefits against the costs. Ask yourself if the debt will contribute to your long-term financial well-being or if it's just a temporary fix for immediate wants or needs. Assessing your current financial situation and determining whether you have the means to repay the debt is also critical.

Additionally, understanding the terms and conditions of any loan agreements or credit cards is essential. Be aware of interest rates, repayment terms, and any fees associated with borrowing. Reading the fine print and asking questions can help you avoid surprises down the road.

6.2 Assessing Your Debt Situation and Creating a Debt Repayment Plan

Debt can be a heavy burden that weighs down on your financial well-being. It can limit your options, cause stress, and hinder your ability to achieve your goals. However, by assessing your debt situation and creating a strategic debt repayment plan, you can take control of your finances and work towards a debt-free future.

To begin the process of assessing your debt situation, gather all relevant information regarding your outstanding debts. This includes credit card statements, loan agreements, and other documents related to your debts. Organize these documents to easily see the total amount owed, interest rates, and minimum monthly payments for each debt.

Once you have a clear picture of your debts, it's important to prioritize them based on factors such as interest rates and outstanding balances. High-interest debts should be prioritized, as they accrue more interest over time and can become a significant financial burden if not addressed promptly.

Next, consider your current financial situation and determine how much you can allocate towards debt repayment each month. Take into account your income, essential expenses, and savings goals. It may be necessary to adjust your budget to free up additional funds for debt repayment.

With this information, you can create a debt repayment plan that suits your circumstances. There are two common approaches to debt repayment: the snowball method and the avalanche method.

The snowball method involves starting with the smallest debt and making extra payments towards it while paying the minimum on all other debts. Once the smallest debt is paid off, the freed-up funds are directed toward the next smallest debt, creating a snowball effect. This method effectively builds momentum and provides a sense of accomplishment as smaller debts are eliminated.

On the other hand, the avalanche method focuses on tackling high-interest debts first. Start by making extra payments towards the debt with the highest interest rate while paying the minimum on other debts. Once the highest-interest debt is paid off, move on to the next highest-interest-rate debt. This method can save you more money in the long run by reducing interest costs.

Choose the method that aligns with your financial goals and motivates you to stay committed to your debt repayment journey. Whichever approach you choose, remember that consistency is critical. Make it a habit to allocate a portion of your monthly income towards debt repayment and celebrate each milestone.

Additionally, consider seeking professional advice if you find yourself struggling to manage your debts or unsure about which repayment strategy is best for you. Financial advisors or credit counseling agencies can provide guidance tailored to your specific situation and help you navigate through challenging circumstances.

6.3 Debt Consolidation Strategies to Simplify Payments and Reduce Interest Rates

Managing debt can be overwhelming and stressful, especially when you have multiple loans or credit card balances to keep track of. One effective strategy to simplify your payments and potentially reduce the amount of interest you pay is debt consolidation.

Debt consolidation involves combining various debts into a single loan or credit line with a lower interest rate. This allows you to make one monthly payment instead of multiple payments to different creditors. Not only does it make managing your debt easier, but it also provides an opportunity to save money on interest charges.

There are several methods you can use to consolidate your debt.

Balance Transfer: If you have high-interest credit card debt, consider transferring the balances to a new credit card with a lower interest rate. Many credit card companies offer promotional periods with zero or low interest rates for balance transfers. However, be cautious of any transfer fees and ensure that you can pay off the balance within the promotional period to avoid accumulating more debt.

Personal Loan: You can take out a personal loan from a bank or online lender to pay off your existing debts. Personal loans often have fixed interest rates and repayment terms, making it easier to budget for the monthly payments. Shop around for the best interest rates and loan terms before committing to a specific lender.

Home Equity Loan or Line of Credit: If you own a home, you may be eligible for a home equity loan or line of credit. These loans allow you to borrow against the equity in your home and use the funds to pay off your debts. Home equity loans generally have lower interest rates compared to credit cards or personal loans. However, remember that your home is collateral, and failing to repay this loan could result in foreclosure.

Debt Management Plan: If your debts have become unmanageable, you may consider enrolling in a debt management plan (DMP) offered by nonprofit credit counseling agencies. A DMP involves working with a credit counselor who negotiates with your creditors to reduce interest rates and consolidate your debts into one monthly payment. While enrolled in a DMP, you will make regular payments to the credit counseling agency, who will distribute the funds to your creditors.

When considering debt consolidation, evaluating the potential benefits and drawbacks is essential. Here are some key points to keep in mind.

Lower Interest Rates: Debt consolidation can help you secure a lower interest rate, reducing the amount of money you spend on interest over time. This can save you substantial amounts of money, especially if you have high-interest credit card debt.

Simplified Repayment: Instead of juggling multiple payments and due dates, debt consolidation allows for a single monthly payment. This simplifies your finances and helps you stay organized.

Extended Repayment Term: Depending on the debt consolidation method you choose, you may extend your repayment term. While this can lower your monthly payments, it may also result in paying more interest over time.

Qualification Requirements: Remember that qualifying for certain types of debt consolidation, such as balance transfers or personal loans, may require a good credit score. If your credit score is low, you may need to find other options or work on improving your credit before consolidating your debts.

Changing Spending Habits: Debt consolidation is not a cure-all solution for financial troubles. It's crucial to address the root causes of your debt and develop responsible spending habits moving forward. Otherwise, consolidating your debts may only provide temporary relief.

Before proceeding with any debt consolidation strategy, take the time to research and compare different options thoroughly. Consider consulting with a financial advisor or credit counselor who can provide personalized guidance based on your unique financial situation.

6.4 Negotiating with Creditors for Better Terms or Debt Settlement Options

When facing a significant amount of debt, negotiating with your creditors can be a powerful tool in regaining control of your financial situation. Many people are unaware that creditors are often willing to work with you to find a solution that benefits both parties. By engaging in open and honest communication, you may be able to secure better terms or even explore debt settlement options.

The first step in negotiating with creditors is to gather all the necessary information about your debts. Make sure you have a clear understanding of the total amount owed, the interest rates, and any additional fees or penalties. This knowledge will help you make informed decisions during negotiations and present specific offers to your creditors.

Next, it's important to approach the negotiation process with confidence and a willingness to find a mutually beneficial solution. Remember, creditors are interested in recovering their money, so they may be open to alternative payment arrangements if it means they can avoid lengthy and costly legal proceedings.

When contacting your creditors, be prepared to explain your current financial situation honestly. Let them know about any hardships you are facing that have contributed to your inability to meet your obligations. This transparency can help them understand your circumstances and make them more willing to negotiate.

During negotiations, proposing realistic solutions based on your financial ability is crucial. For example, you might suggest lower interest rates, extended repayment periods, or reduced monthly payments. Be prepared to provide evidence of your financial situation, such as pay stubs or bank statements, to support your claims.

If you find yourself struggling to negotiate with your creditors directly, consider enlisting the help of a reputable credit counseling agency. These organizations have experience working with creditors and can advocate on your behalf. They may be able to negotiate better terms or assist in setting up a debt management plan that consolidates your payments into one affordable monthly sum.

Alternatively, suppose you are experiencing extreme financial hardship and cannot repay your debts in full. In that case, debt settlement may be an option worth exploring. Debt settlement involves negotiating with creditors to accept a lump-sum payment that is less than the total amount owed. This can significantly reduce the burden of debt but should only be considered after careful consideration and consultation with professionals.

6.5 Maintaining Good Credit While Repaying Debt

Maintaining a good credit score is essential, even while you are focused on repaying your debt. Your credit score significantly affects your financial health and can impact future borrowing opportunities. Here are some strategies to help you manage your debt while maintaining a positive credit history.

Pay your bills on time: Timely payments are crucial for maintaining a good credit score. Missing or making late payments can negatively affect your creditworthiness. Set up reminders or automatic payments to ensure you never miss a due date.

Prioritize high-interest debts: While making minimum payments on all your debts is important, consider directing extra funds towards high-interest debts first. Paying off these debts faster will save you money in interest charges and help improve your credit utilization ratio.

Communicate with creditors: If you're struggling to meet your payment obligations, don't hesitate to contact your creditors. Many lenders are willing to work with you. They may offer temporary solutions, such as reduced interest rates or payment plans, to help ease your financial burden.

Avoid opening new credit accounts: While it may be tempting to open new credit accounts to help with your debt repayment, doing so can hurt your credit score. Opening new accounts can lower the average age of your credit history and increase the number of recent inquiries on your report.

Regularly review your credit report: Monitor your credit report regularly to ensure there are no errors or discrepancies that could negatively impact your credit score. If you find any inaccuracies, contact the credit reporting agencies to have them corrected.

Use credit responsibly: As you work toward paying off your debts, use credit responsibly. Only make purchases that you can afford to pay off in full each month. This demonstrates responsible credit management and can positively contribute to your credit score.

Consider professional help if needed: If you're overwhelmed by your debt situation or struggling to manage it alone, consider contacting a credit counseling agency or a reputable debt consolidation company. These professionals can guide and assist in developing a plan to repay your debts while protecting your credit.

6.6 Long-term Strategies for Avoiding Future Debt and Improving Financial Health

Now that you have developed a plan to repay your current debts, it is important to implement long-term strategies to avoid falling into the debt cycle again. By being proactive and making smart financial decisions, you can improve your overall financial health and reduce the likelihood of accumulating new debt.

One of the first steps towards avoiding future debt is to create a realistic budget and stick to it. Your budget should reflect your income, expenses, and savings goals. It should also include a contingency fund for unexpected expenses. By tracking your spending and being mindful of your financial goals, you can ensure that you live within your means and not rely on credit to make ends meet.

Another key strategy is to build an emergency fund. Life is full of surprises, and having a financial cushion can help you navigate through unexpected expenses without turning to credit cards or loans. Aim to save at least three to six months' living expenses in your emergency fund. This will provide you with a safety net and give you peace of mind, knowing that you are financially prepared for any unforeseen circumstances.

Furthermore, it is essential to differentiate between needs and wants. Many people fall into debt because they confuse their wants with their needs. Take the time to evaluate whether a purchase is necessary or simply a desire that can be postponed or eliminated altogether. By being mindful of your spending habits and prioritizing your needs over your wants, you can avoid unnecessary debt and maintain a healthy financial balance.

Additionally, developing healthy financial habits can significantly contribute to avoiding future debt. This includes paying bills on time, avoiding unnecessary credit card usage, and regularly reviewing your financial statements for any discrepancies or fraudulent activity. You can prevent costly mistakes and predatory lending practices by staying organized and disciplined in your financial management.

Education and knowledge are also powerful tools in avoiding future debt. Stay informed about personal finance topics such as interest rates, credit scores, and investment options. Continuously educate yourself on financial literacy to make informed decisions regarding borrowing money, investing, and saving for the future.

Finally, seek support from professionals or support groups if needed. Financial advisors or counselors can provide guidance tailored to your specific situation and help you navigate through challenging financial decisions. Joining support groups or online communities focused on personal finance can also provide valuable insights and encouragement from individuals who have successfully overcome debt and achieved financial stability.

6.7 Wrapping It Up

In this chapter, we delved into the topic of debt management. We discovered effective strategies for breaking free from the debt cycle. We began by understanding the different types of debt and their implications on our financial health. By assessing our individual debt situation, we were able to create a personalized debt repayment plan that suited our needs and goals.

We discussed the concept of debt consolidation and how it can simplify our payments and reduce interest rates. Through negotiation with creditors, we explored options for better terms or even debt settlement. Maintaining good credit while repaying debt is crucial, and we learned valuable tips on how to do so.

However, our journey towards financial freedom does not end with debt repayment. We also focused on long-term strategies for avoiding future debt and improving our overall financial health. By adopting responsible borrowing habits and practicing good financial management skills, we can prevent falling back into the cycle of debt.

Remember, breaking free from debt requires discipline, commitment, and resilience. It may not be easy, but with determination and the tools provided in this chapter, you can overcome your debts and achieve financial independence.

As we wrap up this chapter on debt management, take a moment to reflect on your own debt situation. What steps can you take today to start paying off your debts? How can you adjust your spending habits to avoid accumulating more debt in the future?

In the next chapter, we will explore the importance of developing healthy spending habits. By understanding the triggers behind impulsive buying behavior and learning strategies to curb it, you can gain control over your finances and make mindful decisions about your spending.

Chapter 7: Developing Healthy Spending Habits

"Too many people spend money they earned…to buy things they don't want…to impress people that they don't like." – Will Rogers

In today's consumer-driven society, it's easy to fall into the trap of impulsive spending and overspending. Everywhere we turn, we are bombarded with advertisements and enticing offers that make us believe we need more, that our lives will be better if we just buy that latest gadget or trendy item. But the truth is, true financial success lies in developing healthy spending habits and being mindful of our purchases.

This chapter will explore the importance of understanding our spending triggers and uncovering the underlying causes of impulsive buying behavior. We will discuss strategies for curbing impulsive spending and creating a realistic spending plan that aligns with our values. We can prioritize necessities over wants by evaluating purchases based on their value and long-term impact and build resilience against persuasive marketing tactics.

It's time to take control of our spending habits and avoid

falling into the endless cycle of accumulating unnecessary debt. By cultivating mindful spending techniques and making responsible consumption choices, we can achieve our financial goals and live a more fulfilling life.

7.1 Identifying Triggers and Underlying Causes of Impulsive Spending

In today's consumer-driven society, it's no surprise that many struggle with impulse buying and overspending. The allure of shiny new gadgets, trendy clothes, and luxurious vacations can be hard to resist. However, understanding the underlying causes of impulsive spending is essential to develop healthier spending habits.

One common trigger for impulsive spending is emotional distress. Many people turn to shopping as a temporary relief or to fill a void in their lives. It's important to recognize that buying material possessions will not address these emotional needs in the long run. Instead, finding healthier coping mechanisms such as self-care, seeking support from loved ones, or engaging in fulfilling hobbies is crucial.

Another trigger for impulsive spending is the influence of advertising and marketing tactics. Companies spend billions of dollars annually on advertising campaigns to persuade consumers to make impulsive purchases. From flashy commercials to enticing sales promotions, these tactics are specifically crafted to exploit our desires and create a sense of urgency. By being aware of these manipulative strategies, we can develop the resilience to resist impulse buying and make more thoughtful purchasing decisions.

Social pressure can also significantly contribute to impulsive spending. We often feel compelled to keep up with friends or societal expectations, leading us to make purchases that may not align with our true values or financial capabilities. It's important to remember that true happiness and fulfillment cannot be measured by material possessions or appearances. Developing a strong sense of self and staying true to our priorities can help us resist the temptation to overspend based on social pressures.

Reflecting on your triggers and examining the underlying causes of your impulsive spending can empower you to take control of your finances. By addressing these triggers head-on and finding healthier alternatives, you can break free from the impulse buying cycle and cultivate more mindful spending habits.

Take the time to reflect on instances when you have succumbed to impulse buying. What emotions were you experiencing at that moment? Were there any external factors that influenced your decision? Understanding the root causes of your impulsive spending will allow you to develop effective strategies for avoiding future pitfalls.

7.2 Strategies for Curbing Impulsive Buying Behavior

Impulse buying can be a significant obstacle to achieving financial stability and reaching your financial goals. It's easy to get caught up in the moment and make impulsive purchases you regret later. However, by implementing specific strategies, you can learn to curb this behavior and develop healthy spending habits.

One effective strategy for curbing impulse buying is creating a waiting period before making non-essential purchases. When you feel the urge to buy something on impulse, force yourself to wait at least 24 hours before making the purchase. This waiting period allows your initial excitement to subside. It allows you to carefully consider whether the item is necessary or aligns with your financial goals and values.

Another strategy is to make a list before going shopping and stick to it. Whether heading to the grocery store or the mall, having a predetermined list of items helps keep you focused on what you need rather than succumbing to the allure of spontaneous purchases. You can avoid unnecessary spending and stay within your budget by sticking to your list.

Additionally, try practicing mindful spending techniques. Before making a purchase, ask yourself if the item is a want or a need. Consider its long-term value and consider how it aligns with your financial goals. By consciously evaluating each purchase, you can prioritize necessities over wants and make more thoughtful decisions about where your money goes.

Evaluating purchases based on their value rather than their price tag is also beneficial. A low-priced item may seem like a good deal at first glance, but it may not be worth the cost if it doesn't serve a practical purpose or bring long-term satisfaction. Instead, focus on investing in value items that contribute to your overall well-being.

Another important skill to develop is resilience against persuasive marketing tactics. Advertisements are designed to trigger emotions and create a sense of urgency, enticing you to make impulsive purchases. By becoming aware of these tactics and understanding how they manipulate consumer behavior, you can better resist their influence and make more informed choices.

Lastly, consider finding alternative activities or hobbies that bring fulfillment without relying on material possessions. Engage in activities such as exercising, reading, spending time with loved ones, or pursuing personal interests. By shifting your focus away from consumerism, you can reduce the desire for impulsive purchases and find contentment in non-material aspects of life.

7.3 Creating a Realistic Spending Plan Aligned with Your Values

To begin, take some time to reflect on your values and what you truly care about in life. Are experiences more important to you than material possessions? Do you value giving back to your community or supporting causes that are meaningful to you? Understanding your values will help guide your financial decisions and allow you to budget in a way that supports what matters most to you.

Once you have identified your values, it's time to create a spending plan that reflects them. Start by listing out all of your necessary expenses, such as housing, food, transportation, and utilities. Include any recurring bills or payments you must make each month.

Next, consider your discretionary expenses—those that are not necessary for survival but contribute to your overall quality of life. These could include things like dining out, entertainment, hobbies, or vacations. Assign a portion of your income to these discretionary expenses based on their importance to you and your financial goals.

It's important to note that while it's essential to budget for discretionary expenses, be mindful of overspending in this category. Take the time to evaluate each expense and consider whether it truly aligns with your values and brings you lasting happiness. Sometimes, we can fall into the trap of impulse buying or indulging in temporary pleasures that do not contribute to our long-term financial well-being.

As you create your spending plan, remember to allocate a portion of your income towards savings and investments. Building an emergency fund and investing for the future are critical components of financial success. Making saving a priority in your budget ensures you build a strong foundation for long-term financial security.

Reviewing and adjusting your spending plan regularly is also vital. Life circumstances change, priorities shift, and unforeseen expenses may arise. By regularly reviewing your budget, you can identify areas for improvement and make necessary adjustments to ensure that your money is working in alignment with your values.

Remember, creating a realistic spending plan is not about depriving yourself or restricting your enjoyment of life. It's about being intentional with every dollar you spend and ensuring that it aligns with what truly brings you happiness and fulfillment. When your spending is aligned with your values, you'll find that managing your money becomes easier and more enjoyable.

Take the time today to reflect on your values and create a spending plan that reflects them. Doing so will give you clarity on what truly matters to you and take control of your financial future.

7.4 Mindful Spending Techniques to Prioritize Necessities over Wants

In today's consumer-driven society, it is easy to fall into the trap of mindless spending. We are constantly bombarded with advertisements and enticing offers that make us believe we need the latest gadgets, trendy clothes, or luxurious vacations. However, developing mindful spending habits can help us differentiate between our wants and our needs, allowing us to make more informed and responsible financial decisions.

Mindful spending is about being conscious of our choices and understanding the true value of our purchases. It involves taking a step back before making a buying decision and asking ourselves important questions such as:

"Is this item a necessity or a want?"

"Will this purchase enhance my life in a meaningful way?"

"Can I afford this without compromising my financial goals?"

"Am I buying this because of peer pressure or societal expectations?"

"Will this purchase align with my values and long-term aspirations?"

By asking these questions, we can gain clarity on whether a particular expense is worth it or if it will hinder our financial progress. Here are some practical mindful spending techniques to prioritize necessities over wants.

Create a realistic spending plan: With a clear budget, you can allocate your money towards essential expenses first. This ensures that your basic needs are met before considering any discretionary purchases.

Practice the 24-hour rule: When you find an item you feel compelled to buy, give yourself at least 24 hours before making the purchase. This time allows you to reflect on whether it aligns with your financial goals and is truly something you need.

Set spending limits: Before shopping or engaging in online browsing, set specific limits for yourself. Determine how much you will spend on non-essential items and stick to that amount.

Identify alternative options: Instead of immediately purchasing a specific brand or product, take some time to research alternatives that may offer similar benefits at a lower cost. This can help you make more cost-effective choices without sacrificing quality.

Practice delayed gratification: Train yourself to delay instant gratification by saving up for larger purchases instead of relying on credit or impulse buying. This helps you become more disciplined and gives you time to evaluate whether the purchase is truly necessary.

Track your emotions: Pay attention to how you feel when buying. Are you feeling stressed, bored, or anxious? Acknowledging these emotions can help you recognize when you use purchases as a coping mechanism and find healthier ways to address those underlying feelings.

Surround yourself with like-minded individuals: Interacting with people who share similar financial values can encourage and support mindful spending habits. Joining online communities or attending local financial workshops can be great opportunities to connect with others on a similar financial journey.

7.5 Evaluating Purchases Based on Value and Long-term Impact

When it comes to spending your hard-earned money, it's important to ensure every purchase is worth it and aligns with your long-term financial goals. This means evaluating each purchase based on its value and considering its impact on your overall financial well-being.

To begin, ask yourself whether the item or service you're

considering purchasing is necessary or more of a want.

"Is this something that will bring lasting value to your life, or is it simply a passing desire?"

By reflecting on these questions, you can determine whether the purchase is worth making.

Next, consider the long-term impact of the purchase.

"Will it contribute to your financial stability and future goals?"

For example, if you're contemplating buying a new car, consider whether the payments and associated expenses will fit within your budget and align with your overall financial plan. It may be wise to reconsider if it will strain your finances or hinder progress towards your goals.

Another important aspect of evaluating purchases is comparing prices and exploring alternative options. Take the time to shop around, research different brands, read reviews, and compare prices online. By doing so, you can ensure that you're getting the best value for your money. Additionally, consider whether there are less expensive alternatives that serve the same purpose. Sometimes, opting for a generic brand or a used item can save you significant money without compromising quality.

It's also essential to consider the long-term costs associated with a purchase. For example, if you're considering buying a house, consider not only the mortgage payments but also the maintenance costs, property taxes, and insurance fees. By considering these factors, you'll have a clearer understanding of the true cost of ownership and whether it fits within your budget.

Lastly, always remember to prioritize your financial goals over short-term gratification. While impulse purchases may provide immediate satisfaction, they often have little long-term value. They can derail your progress toward financial stability. Instead of giving in to impulsive urges, consider how the purchase will contribute to your overall financial well-being.

7.6 Building Resilience against Persuasive Marketing Tactics

Today's consumer-driven society constantly bombards us with persuasive marketing tactics to entice us into making unnecessary purchases. From flashy advertisements to clever sales techniques, it can be challenging to resist the allure of these strategies. However, building resilience against such tactics is crucial for maintaining healthy spending habits and achieving financial success.

1. Recognize the manipulation: The first step in building resilience against persuasive marketing tactics is recognizing when you are being manipulated. Advertisers often employ emotional appeals, scarcity tactics, and social proof to convince us that we need their products or services. By understanding these techniques and being mindful of their influence, you can begin to make more informed purchasing decisions.

2. Identify your triggers: Everyone has unique triggers that prompt impulsive buying behavior. It could be feelings of stress, boredom, or even just seeing a sale sign. Take some time to reflect on what triggers your desire to spend money frivolously. Once you identify these triggers, you can develop strategies to address them effectively.

3. Practice delayed gratification: One effective strategy for resisting impulse buying is practicing delayed gratification. Before making a purchase, give yourself a cooling-off period of at least 24 hours. During this time, ask yourself if the item is truly necessary and aligns with your financial goals and values. Chances are, you will find that many purchases lose their appeal after some reflection.

4. Set spending limits: Another way to build resilience against persuasive marketing tactics is to set your spending limits. Determine the maximum amount you will spend on non-essential items each month and stick to it. This will prevent impulsive overspending and keep you accountable for your financial goals.

5. Embrace minimalism: In a world obsessed with material possessions, embracing minimalism can be a powerful antidote to persuasive marketing tactics. By adopting a minimalist mindset, you focus on quality over quantity and prioritize experiences and relationships over material goods. This shift in perspective allows you to resist the constant pressure to accumulate more belongings and instead find contentment in living with less.

6. Seek out alternative sources of fulfillment: Our desire to make impulsive purchases often stems from a deeper longing for fulfillment or satisfaction in our lives. By seeking out alternative sources of fulfillment, such as hobbies, relationships, or personal growth activities, you can reduce the reliance on material possessions for happiness. Engaging in activities that align with your values and bring you joy will help diminish the appeal of persuasive marketing tactics.

7. Foster a supportive environment: Building resilience against persuasive marketing tactics is easier when surrounded by like-minded individuals who support your financial goals. Seek out friends or family members who prioritize mindful spending and share your commitment to financial empowerment. Together, you can encourage and motivate each other to resist the allure of unnecessary purchases.

7.7 Wrapping It Up

In this chapter, we have delved into the world of spending habits and explored ways to avoid impulse buying and overspending. We have learned that impulsive spending can affect our financial well-being and hinder our progress toward achieving our financial goals. However, by understanding the triggers and underlying causes of impulsive spending, we can develop strategies to curb this behavior and regain control over our finances.

One of the key strategies we discussed was creating a realistic spending plan that aligns with our values. By consciously evaluating our purchases based on their value and long-term impact, we can prioritize necessities over wants and make more informed choices about how we spend our money. Mindful spending techniques, such as waiting 24 hours before making a purchase or setting a budget for discretionary expenses, also effectively curb impulsive buying tendencies.

Throughout this chapter, we have emphasized the importance of building resilience against persuasive marketing tactics. By understanding the tactics advertisers and marketers use, we can become more discerning consumers and avoid falling prey to their manipulation. It is crucial to stay focused on our financial goals and resist the temptation to make impulsive purchases that do not align with our long-term objectives.

As we conclude this chapter, it is essential to remember that developing healthy spending habits is an ongoing process. Consistent effort and self-awareness are required to overcome the allure of impulsive buying. By continuously evaluating our spending patterns and reflecting on our financial goals, we can ensure that our money is used wisely and purposefully.

In the next chapter, we will explore the fundamentals of credit and responsible borrowing. Understanding the role of credit in our financial lives is crucial for building a strong foundation for long-term financial success. We will delve into topics such as credit scores, managing credit cards, and strategies for improving creditworthiness. Stay tuned as we continue our journey towards mastering money skills and achieving financial independence.

Chapter 8: Understanding Credit

"Credit is a powerful tool that can either build you up or tear you down. It all depends on how you wield it."

In today's world, credit plays a significant role in our financial lives. Whether buying a car, purchasing a home, or even starting a business, many of our financial goals require access to credit. However, credit can be a double-edged sword, either propelling us towards our dreams or leading us into a cycle of debt and financial instability. Understanding credit and using it responsibly is essential for anyone seeking financial success.

This chapter delves deep into the world of credit, providing you with the knowledge and tools to navigate this complex terrain. Through a blend of informative content, personal experience-based insights, and practical guidance, this chapter aims to demystify credit and empower you to make informed decisions about borrowing.

We will explore the importance of credit scores and reports with vivid descriptions and step-by-step explanations. By understanding the key factors affecting your creditworthiness, you will gain the ability to establish and manage credit responsibly.

This chapter will guide you through various aspects of credit management, including responsible credit card usage, interest rates, fees, penalties, and strategies for improving your credit score. We will also discuss the intricacies of intelligently navigating credit applications, loans, and mortgages.

By the end of this chapter, you will possess a comprehensive understanding of credit that will enable you to make informed borrowing decisions aligned with your long-term financial goals. Armed with this knowledge, you will be equipped to leverage credit to build wealth and secure your financial future.

8.1 The Importance of Credit Scores and Reports

When it comes to personal finance, understanding credit scores and reports is crucial. Your credit score is a three-digit number representing your creditworthiness in the eyes of lenders and financial institutions. It significantly determines whether you will be approved for loans, credit cards, or even rental applications.

On the other hand, your credit report is a detailed record of your financial history, including information about your loans, credit cards, payment history, and any outstanding debts. It provides a comprehensive overview of your financial behavior and is the basis for calculating your credit score.

Having a good credit score opens doors to favorable financial opportunities. It can result in lower interest rates on loans, higher credit limits on credit cards, and more favorable terms when applying for mortgages or car loans. On the contrary, a poor credit score can limit your access to credit or result in higher interest rates and fees, ultimately costing you more money in the long run.

To maintain a good credit score, you should understand what factors affect it. Payment history, which accounts for about 35% of your score, refers to whether you make payments on time. Missed or late payments can negatively impact your credit score.

Another significant factor is your utilization ratio, which makes up approximately 30% of your score. This ratio reflects the percentage of available credit you use at any given time. Keeping this ratio low demonstrates responsible credit usage and positively impacts your score.

Other factors include the length of your credit history (15%), types of credit used (10%), and recent inquiries for new credit (10%). Understanding how these factors contribute to your overall creditworthiness can help you make informed financial decisions that will positively impact your credit score.

It's important to regularly monitor your credit reports to ensure accuracy and identify any potential errors or identity theft. By law, you are entitled to one free copy of your credit report from each of the three major credit bureaus (Equifax, Experian, and TransUnion) annually. Take advantage of this opportunity to review your reports for any discrepancies and address them promptly.

Improving your credit score requires discipline and responsible borrowing habits. Paying bills on time, keeping credit card balances low, and avoiding excessive new credit applications are all effective ways to build and maintain good credit.

8.2 Establishing Credit Responsibly

Establishing a good credit history is essential for achieving financial success and obtaining favorable terms on future loans or lines of credit. Your credit score is a snapshot of your creditworthiness, indicating how likely you are to repay borrowed money. Whether you're applying for a mortgage, car loan, or even renting an apartment, your credit history will be reviewed to determine your eligibility.

It's important to understand the key factors contributing to your credit score. Payment history carries the most weight, accounting for approximately 35% of your overall score. Making all of your payments on time is crucial in building a positive credit history.

One way to begin establishing credit is by opening a secured credit card. Secured credit cards require a cash deposit as collateral for the credit limit. It allows individuals with little or no credit history to build credit by making small purchases and paying them off in full each month.

Another option is becoming an authorized user on someone else's credit card account. By doing so, you can benefit from their positive payment history and strengthen your own credit profile. However, it's important to choose someone who has a responsible approach to credit and who will not jeopardize your financial well-being.

Properly managing your credit utilization ratio is another key factor in establishing credit responsibly. This ratio compares the amount of credit you use to the total amount available to you. Keeping your utilization below 30% demonstrates responsible borrowing habits and can positively impact your credit score.

Monitoring your credit report regularly for errors or discrepancies is also advisable. Once per year, you can request a free copy of your credit report from each of the three major credit bureaus—Equifax, Experian, and TransUnion. Review the report thoroughly and dispute any inaccuracies promptly to ensure the information being reported is accurate.

Lastly, be cautious when applying for new lines of credit. Each application creates a hard inquiry on your credit report, which can temporarily lower your score. Only apply for credit when necessary and avoid opening multiple accounts within a short period of time.

8.3 Managing Credit Cards Wisely

Credit cards can be powerful financial tools when used responsibly. They offer convenience, flexibility, and the potential to build a positive credit history. However, if mismanaged, they can lead to debt and financial stress.

First and foremost, it is essential to understand how credit cards work. When you make a purchase with a credit card, you are essentially borrowing money from the card issuer. It is crucial to remember that this borrowed money needs to be repaid in full by the due date to avoid interest charges.

To manage your credit cards effectively, consider these key tips.

Pay your balance in full: Make it a habit to pay off your credit card balance in full every month. This will prevent interest charges and allow you to fully enjoy the benefits of using a credit card without falling into debt.

Avoid unnecessary purchases: Use your credit card only for planned purchases or emergencies. Avoid impulsive buying behavior and evaluate whether you need an item before charging it to your card.

Set spending limits: Based on your budget and financial goals, establish clear spending limits for each credit card you own. Stick to these limits and avoid exceeding them unless necessary.

Monitor your statements: Regularly review your credit card statements to ensure all charges are accurate and authorized. You can protect yourself from financial harm by promptly addressing any discrepancies or fraudulent activity.

Utilize rewards programs: Many credit cards offer rewards that allow you to earn points or cash back on your purchases. Take advantage of these programs, but be cautious not to overspend just to accumulate rewards.

Keep track of due dates: Missing credit card payments can result in late fees and damage your credit score. Set up reminders or automatic payments to ensure that you never miss a payment deadline.

Limit the number of credit cards: Having multiple credit cards can make it challenging to keep track of your spending and manage your payments effectively. Consider consolidating your cards and only keeping those that serve your specific needs.

Responsible credit card management involves using credit cards as a tool for convenience and building credit, not as a means to live beyond one's means. By following these strategies and being mindful of how you use your credit cards, you can maintain financial control and avoid unnecessary debt.

8.4 Understanding Interest Rates, Fees, and Penalties

When it comes to borrowing money, whether through credit cards, loans, or mortgages, it's crucial to have a solid understanding of interest rates, fees, and penalties. These factors can significantly impact your overall financial health and should not be underestimated.

Interest rates are the percentage of the loan amount you'll pay on top of the principal. They can vary depending on several factors, such as your credit score, the type of loan, and market conditions. It's important to shop around and compare interest rates from different lenders to ensure you're getting the best deal possible.

Fees are additional charges imposed by lenders for certain services related to borrowing. Examples include origination fees, which are charged when a loan is granted, and late payment fees, which are imposed when you fail to make payments on time. It's essential to read and understand the terms and conditions of any loan agreement to identify potential fees and factor them into your overall borrowing costs.

Penalties are consequences that borrowers may face if they violate the terms of their loan agreement. These can include late payment penalties, prepayment penalties (charged for paying off a loan early), or penalties for exceeding credit limits on credit cards. It's crucial to be aware of these penalties and adhere to your loan agreement's terms to avoid incurring unnecessary costs.

8.5 Strategies for Improving Credit Score

Your credit score plays a vital role in your financial health and future opportunities. A good credit score can open doors to better interest rates on loans, higher credit limits, and greater financial stability. On the other hand, a poor credit score can limit your options and make it difficult to secure loans or even rent an apartment. Fortunately, there are strategies you can implement to improve your credit score and set yourself up for future success.

Pay your bills on time: One of the most important factors in determining your credit score is your payment history. Late payments or missed payments can have a significant negative impact on your score. Make it a priority to pay all your bills on time, whether it's your credit card bill, utility bills, or loan payments. Consider setting up automatic payments or reminders to ensure you never miss a due date.

Reduce your credit utilization ratio: Your credit utilization ratio is the percentage of available credit you are currently using. High credit utilization can negatively impact your credit score. Aim to keep your credit utilization below 30% of your available credit. Paying off debt and lowering your balances can help improve this ratio and demonstrate responsible borrowing habits.

Avoid opening unnecessary new accounts: Opening multiple new accounts within a short period of time can raise red flags to lenders and potentially lower your credit score. Only apply for new credit when necessary, and be selective about the types of accounts you open.

Diversify your credit mix: Having a mix of different types of credit (such as credit cards, loans, and mortgages) can positively impact your credit score. It demonstrates that you can handle various types of debt responsibly. If you only have one type of credit, consider diversifying by responsibly adding another type of credit to your financial portfolio.

Review your credit report regularly: Mistakes on your credit report can negatively impact your score without you even realizing it. Regularly reviewing your credit report allows you to identify errors or discrepancies and dispute them with the credit bureaus. You are entitled to one free copy of your credit report from each of the three major credit bureaus every year.

Use caution when closing old accounts: Closing old accounts may seem like a good idea to simplify your financial life; however, it can actually harm your credit score. The length of your credit history is an important factor in determining your score, so closing old accounts can shorten the average age of your accounts. If you decide to close an account, prioritize closing newer ones first.

Seek professional guidance if needed: If your credit score is severely damaged or you're struggling with debt, don't hesitate to seek professional advice from a reputable credit counseling agency. They can provide guidance specific to your situation and help you develop a plan for improving your credit score.

8.6 Navigating Credit Applications, Loans, and Mortgages

Once you have established a solid foundation of responsible borrowing and have a good understanding of credit, it's time to navigate the world of credit applications, loans, and mortgages. These financial tools can help you achieve your goals and make significant purchases, but they also come with important considerations you must be aware of.

When applying for credit, whether it's a credit card, personal loan, or mortgage, it's crucial to do your research and compare different options. Look for competitive interest rates, favorable terms, and any additional fees or charges that may apply. Remember, the goal is to find the most suitable credit product that aligns with your financial goals and situation.

Before committing to any credit agreement, take the time to read through the terms and conditions carefully. Understand the repayment schedule, interest rate calculations, and any penalties for late payments or early repayment. By being fully informed, you can avoid any unpleasant surprises down the line.

When it comes to loans, whether they are personal loans or student loans, consider your needs carefully. Assess how much you truly need to borrow and evaluate your ability to repay the loan comfortably. Avoid taking on more debt than necessary, and strive to find the most reasonable repayment plan that fits within your budget.

Mortgages warrant special attention as they involve much larger sums of money over extended periods of time. Before beginning the home-buying process, calculate how much house you can afford based on your income and other financial obligations. Keep in mind that there are costs beyond the purchase price of a home, such as closing costs and ongoing maintenance expenses.

Additionally, research different types of mortgages and their respective pros and cons. Fixed-rate mortgages offer stability with predictable monthly payments. In contrast, adjustable-rate mortgages may provide lower initial rates but carry the risk of fluctuating payments in the future. Consult with a mortgage professional who can guide you through the process and help you make an informed decision.

Remember that applying for credit, loans, or mortgages will impact your credit score. Each application will result in a hard inquiry on your credit report, which can temporarily lower your score. Therefore, it's important to be selective about the credit applications you submit and only pursue those that you genuinely need.

Building a positive credit history requires responsible borrowing and timely repayments. Continue managing your credit wisely even after obtaining new credit or loans. Pay your bills on time, keep your balances low relative to your credit limits, and avoid opening unnecessary lines of credit.

8.7 Wrapping It Up

In this chapter, we delved into the world of credit. We explored the importance of understanding how it can impact our financial well-being. We discussed the significance of credit scores and reports, as well as the steps to establish credit responsibly. By managing credit cards wisely, we can avoid falling into debt traps and ensure that our borrowing habits support our overall financial goals.

We also took a closer look at interest rates, fees, and penalties associated with credit. Understanding these factors is crucial in making informed decisions about borrowing money and avoiding unnecessary costs. By implementing strategies for improving credit scores, such as paying bills on time and keeping credit utilization low, we can enhance our financial standing and open up more opportunities for favorable lending terms.

Navigating credit applications, loans, and mortgages can be intimidating, but armed with the knowledge from this chapter, you now have the tools to make informed choices. We discussed the importance of shopping around for the best rates and terms and the significance of reading and understanding loan agreements thoroughly.

Remember, responsible borrowing is key to maintaining a healthy financial life. By being mindful of your borrowing habits and using credit as a tool rather than a crutch, you can build a solid foundation for long-term financial success.

As we wrap up this chapter, I encourage you to reflect on your current credit situation. Review your credit reports, assess your debt-to-income ratio, and evaluate your overall creditworthiness. Use the information provided in this chapter to develop a plan for improving your credit or maintaining your already good standing.

In the next chapter, we will explore another critical aspect of personal finance – insurance. Understanding different types of insurance coverage and ensuring adequate protection for yourself and your assets is crucial in securing your financial future.

Chapter 9: Insurance

"Insurance is not about getting rich quick, it's about avoiding becoming poor slowly."

Insurance is an essential aspect of personal finance that often gets overlooked or misunderstood. Many underestimate the importance of protecting themselves and their assets from unforeseen circumstances and potential financial losses. However, as the quote above suggests, insurance can be seen as a means to safeguard against the risks that life presents.

In this chapter, we will delve into the world of insurance and its significance in achieving financial security. We will explore the different types of insurance coverage available and how they can act as a safety net during times of uncertainty. We will also discuss strategies for assessing your insurance needs based on your circumstances and finding the right policies that provide adequate coverage at affordable premiums.

Understanding the importance of insurance goes beyond simply acquiring policies; it involves evaluating risks, comparing providers, and maximizing the benefits received from insurance coverage. Therefore, throughout this chapter, we will discuss the various types of insurance and guide how to make informed decisions regarding coverage options.

By the end of this chapter, you will have a comprehensive understanding of insurance fundamentals and be equipped with the knowledge to effectively protect yourself and your assets.

9.1 Understanding the Different Types of Insurance Coverage

Insurance plays a crucial role in protecting ourselves and our assets from unforeseen events. Understanding the different types of insurance coverage available can help us make informed decisions about our financial well-being.

One of the most common types of insurance is health insurance, which covers medical expenses and provides access to healthcare services. It ensures financial protection in case of illness, injury, or unexpected medical emergencies. Health insurance plans vary in terms of coverage and cost, so it's essential to carefully evaluate different options to find the right fit for our needs.

Another critical type of insurance is auto insurance, which protects both ourselves and others in case of accidents or damages involving our vehicles. Auto insurance typically includes liability coverage, which pays for injuries or property damage caused to others, as well as collision and comprehensive coverage, which covers repairs or replacements for our vehicle. The specific coverage options may vary depending on local regulations and individual preferences.

Homeowners' or renters' insurance protects our homes or rental properties against risks such as fire, theft, or natural disasters. This type of insurance covers the structure itself. It includes coverage for personal belongings and liability in case someone gets injured on the property. It's important to understand our policy's specific terms and conditions to ensure we have adequate coverage for our unique circumstances.

Life insurance is designed to provide financial support for our loved ones in the event of our death. It offers a lump-sum payment or regular income to beneficiaries, ensuring they have financial stability even when we're no longer there to provide for them. Life insurance policies come in various forms, including term life insurance (providing coverage for a specified period) and permanent life insurance (providing lifelong coverage with potential cash value accumulation).

Additionally, specialized types of insurance cater to specific needs and situations. These include disability insurance, which replaces a portion of our income if we become unable to work due to injury or illness, and long-term care insurance, which helps cover the high costs associated with extended care services such as nursing homes or assisted living facilities.

9.2 Assessing Insurance Needs Based on Individual Circumstances

Insurance plays a crucial role in protecting ourselves and our assets from unexpected events. However, it can be confusing to determine what type and amount of insurance coverage is necessary for each individual. Assessing insurance needs based on individual circumstances is essential in ensuring adequate protection while avoiding unnecessary expenses.

The first step in assessing insurance needs is to evaluate your current financial situation and identify any potential risks or vulnerabilities. Consider factors such as your age, health condition, occupation, and lifestyle choices. For example, suppose you have dependents who rely on your income. In that case, life insurance should be a priority to ensure their financial security in the event of your untimely demise.

Next, consider your assets and their value. Do you own a home? Have you invested in valuable personal belongings such as jewelry or artwork? Evaluating the replacement cost or potential loss associated with these assets will guide you in deciding the appropriate coverage limits for homeowner's or renter's insurance and additional policies such as umbrella insurance or valuable items coverage.

Another important aspect to consider when assessing insur-ance needs is your level of risk tolerance. Some individuals may prefer comprehensive coverage that protects against a wide range of risks, while others may opt for more minimal coverage to reduce premiums. Understanding your comfort level with risk will help you make informed decisions about the types and amounts of insurance coverage you require.

Additionally, think about the potential impact of deductibles and out-of-pocket expenses on your finances. Higher deductibles generally result in lower premiums but require you to pay more out of pocket before insurance coverage kicks in. Analyzing your financial ability to handle unexpected expenses will help you strike the right balance between affordable premiums and manageable deductibles.

It is also advisable to consider any legal requirements for insurance coverage. For example, auto insurance is mandatory in most states, and failing to comply with this requirement can lead to penalties and legal consequences. Stay informed about the specific insurance requirements relevant to your circumstances and ensure compliance to avoid unnecessary risks.

Lastly, consulting with an insurance professional can provide valuable insights into your unique insurance needs. These professionals can assess your individual circumstances, recommend appropriate coverage options, and provide cost estimates. They can also help you navigate complex insurance terms and conditions, ensuring you fully understand the scope of coverage and potential exclusions.

9.3 Comparing Insurance Providers and Policies

When it comes to selecting insurance coverage, it is essential to compare different providers and policies to ensure you are getting the best value for your money. Insurance is a critical aspect of personal finance, as it offers protection against unforeseen events and mitigates potential financial losses.

To compare insurance providers and policies effectively, follow these steps.

1. Research multiple providers: Start by researching different insurance companies that offer coverage in the areas you need. Look for reputable companies with strong financial stability and a good track record of customer satisfaction. Online reviews and ratings can be helpful in assessing the reputation and reliability of insurance providers.

2. Assess coverage options: Understand the types of coverage each provider offers and determine which ones align with your specific needs. Common types of insurance include health, auto, home, life, disability, and liability insurance. It is crucial to evaluate the extent of coverage provided by each policy and ensure it meets your requirements.

3. Compare premiums: While price should not be the sole factor in choosing an insurance policy, it is essential to compare premiums to ensure they are reasonable and within your budget. Consider the deductible amounts and their impact on the premium costs. Remember that a lower premium may result in higher out-of-pocket expenses in case of a claim.

4. Review policy terms and conditions: Carefully read the terms and conditions of each policy to understand its limitations, exclusions, and coverage limits. Pay attention to any additional fees or penalties associated with the policy. It is vital to clearly understand what is covered and what is not.

5. Evaluate customer service and claims process: Look into each insurance company's quality of customer service. Check if they have a reliable claims process and prompt settlement record. A responsive and efficient claims process can make a significant difference when you need to file a claim.

6. Seek recommendations and advice: Consult with friends, family, or financial advisors who have experience dealing with insurance providers. Their insights can help you make an informed decision based on their firsthand experiences.

7. Consider bundling policies: Many insurance companies offer discounts when you bundle multiple policies, such as combining home and auto insurance or purchasing life insurance and other coverage. Bundling can help save money while ensuring comprehensive coverage across various aspects of your life.

8. Read the fine print: Always read the entire policy document before making a final decision. Make sure you understand all terms, conditions, and exclusions mentioned in the policy. If there are any ambiguous clauses or unclear language, seek clarification from the insurance provider.

9. Seek professional advice if needed: If you find it challenging

to navigate through different insurance policies or need assistance in determining the right coverage for your specific needs,
consider consulting with an independent insurance agent or
financial advisor. They can provide personalized guidance
based on your circumstances.

9.4 Ensuring Adequate Coverage at Affordable Premiums

Having insurance is a crucial part of your overall financial plan.
It provides protection against unexpected events that can have
a devastating impact on your finances. However, it's essential
to ensure that you have adequate coverage without breaking
the bank on high premiums.

When determining the right insurance coverage for your needs,
there are a few key factors to consider. First, assess your
individual circumstances and identify the risks you face. For
example, if you own a home, you'll want to have homeowners
insurance to protect against potential damage or loss. If you
have dependents, life insurance can provide financial support
to your loved ones in the event of your passing.

Next, compare insurance providers and policies to find the
best fit for your needs. Look for reputable companies with
excellent customer service and reliable claims handling. Take
the time to research different policies and understand the
specific coverage they offer. This will help you find the balance
between adequate coverage and affordability.

While it's tempting to cut corners on insurance costs, be

cautious about sacrificing essential coverage just to save a few dollars. While low premiums may seem appealing initially, inadequate coverage can lead to significant financial hardship if an unexpected event occurs. Instead, focus on finding ways to make insurance more affordable without compromising on essential coverage.

One strategy to lower premiums is to increase deductibles. A deductible is the amount you must pay out of pocket before your insurance coverage kicks in. By choosing a higher deductible, you may be able to reduce your monthly premium. Just be sure that the deductible amount is something you can comfortably afford in case of a claim.

Another way to save on insurance costs is by bundling multiple policies with the same company. Many insurance providers offer discounts for purchasing multiple types of coverage from them. For example, you could combine your auto and home insurance policies to take advantage of a multi-policy discount.

Additionally, consider speaking with an independent insurance agent who can shop around on your behalf. These agents work with various insurance companies and can help find the best coverage options at competitive rates.

Review your insurance policies regularly to ensure they still meet your needs. As your circumstances change over time, it's essential to update your coverage accordingly. For example, suppose you've paid off your mortgage. In that case, you may need less homeowners insurance since you no longer need coverage for the structure itself.

While insurance is essential for protecting yourself and your assets, it's crucial to balance adequate coverage with affordable premiums. Assess your individual circumstances, compare policies and providers, and customize your coverage based on your specific needs. Explore strategies like increasing deductibles and bundling policies to lower costs without sacrificing critical protection. Regularly review your policies and make updates as necessary to ensure continued suitability. Remember, having peace of mind through proper insurance coverage is worth the investment in your financial well-being.

9.5 Evaluating Risks and Mitigating Potential Losses

One key aspect of personal finance is protecting yourself and your assets from unexpected risks and losses. Insurance plays a vital role in providing financial security and peace of mind, but it's crucial to ensure you have adequate coverage at affordable premiums.

First, it's important to understand the different types of insurance coverage available. Common types include health insurance, auto insurance, homeowners' or renters' insurance, life insurance, disability insurance, and liability insurance. Each type serves a unique purpose and provides coverage for specific risks.

Assessing your insurance needs involves considering your individual circumstances and identifying the potential risks you may face. For example, if you own a home, homeowners insurance is essential to protect against damage or loss due to events like fire, theft, or natural disasters. If you have a family depending on your income, life insurance can provide financial support in the event of your passing.

Comparing insurance providers and policies is important to ensure you get the best coverage at the most reasonable cost. It's recommended to obtain quotes from multiple insurers and carefully review the terms and conditions of each policy. Pay attention to factors such as coverage limits, deductibles, exclusions, and claim processes.

When evaluating risks, it's essential to balance adequate coverage and affordability. While it may be tempting to opt for minimal coverage to save on premiums, doing so could leave you exposed to significant financial losses in the event of an unforeseen incident. It's important to carefully consider your risk tolerance and determine the level of coverage that aligns with your comfort level.

Mitigating potential losses involves taking proactive measures to minimize risks. This can include implementing safety measures in your home or automobile, such as installing smoke detectors or anti-theft devices, which may result in lower premiums. Maintaining a good credit score can also positively impact your insurance rates.

Periodically reviewing your insurance coverage is essential to ensure it remains up-to-date and aligned with your current needs. Life changes such as marriage, having children, purchasing new assets, or starting a business may require adjustments to your coverage levels.

In the unfortunate event that you need to make an insurance claim, proper claims management is crucial. Promptly reporting any incidents to your insurer and providing accurate documentation will help streamline the claims process and ensure a smooth resolution.

9.6 Maximizing Insurance Benefits Through Proper Claims Management

Proper claims management is vital in maximizing the benefits of your insurance coverage. When unfortunate events occur, and you need to file a claim, understanding the claims process and taking proactive steps can ensure a smooth and successful outcome.

1. Notify your insurance provider promptly: As soon as an incident occurs that may be covered by your insurance policy, notify your insurance provider immediately. This will initiate the claims process and allow them to guide you through the necessary steps.

2. Document the incident: Take detailed notes and gather any evidence related to the incident. This may include photographs, police reports, medical records, or any other relevant documentation. These records will serve as proof when filing your claim.

3. Understand your policy coverage: Familiarize yourself with the terms and conditions of your insurance policy. Each policy may have specific requirements or exclusions that can impact your claim. Knowing what is covered and what isn't will help you navigate the process more efficiently.

4. Provide accurate and complete information: When filing a claim, ensure that all information provided is accurate and complete. Any discrepancies or missing details may lead to delays or possible denial of your claim. Be transparent and honest throughout the process.

5. Follow up regularly: Stay engaged with your insurance provider throughout the claims process. Follow up regularly to inquire about the progress of your claim, ask for updates, and clarify any concerns or questions you may have.

6. Keep track of communication: Maintain a record of all communication with your insurance provider regarding your claim. This includes emails, phone calls, and letters exchanged. A documented conversation history can serve as a reference if any issues arise later.

7. Seek professional assistance if needed: If you encounter any challenges or complexities during the claims process, consider seeking professional assistance from an attorney or public adjuster specializing in insurance claims. They can provide guidance and advocate on your behalf to ensure fair treatment.

8. Review the settlement offer carefully: Once your insurance provider presents a settlement offer, review it carefully. Ensure that it aligns with the terms of your policy and adequately compensates you for your losses. If needed, negotiate with your provider to seek a fair resolution.

9. Appeal if necessary: If you believe your claim was unfairly denied or undervalued, familiarize yourself with the appeals process outlined in your policy. Follow the necessary steps to challenge the decision and present additional evidence or arguments supporting your claim.

9.7 Wrapping It Up

In this chapter, we explored the importance of insurance in protecting ourselves and our assets. We discussed the different types of insurance coverage available and how to assess our individual insurance needs based on our circumstances. By comparing insurance providers and policies, we can ensure that we have adequate coverage at affordable premiums.

Understanding risks and mitigating potential losses is essential in maximizing insurance benefits. We learned about the importance of evaluating risks and taking steps to minimize them. We can make the most out of our insurance coverage by managing claims effectively.

Insurance is not just a safety net but an integral part of our overall financial plan. By securing the right insurance policies, we can protect ourselves from unforeseen events and safeguard our financial stability.

As we wrap up this chapter, remember that insurance is not a one-time decision. Regular evaluations are required to ensure our coverage aligns with our current situation. Stay informed about any changes in your circumstances that may affect your insurance needs and any updates in the insurance industry or laws.

We are securing a more stable future by taking proactive steps to protect ourselves and our assets through insurance. In the next chapter, we will delve into the world of investing and explore strategies for growing our wealth over time.

Chapter 10: Investing Basics

"Compound interest is the eighth wonder of the world. He who understands it, earns it... he who doesn't... pays it." - Albert Einstein

Investing is often considered an elusive concept, reserved for the wealthy or those with specialized knowledge. However, the truth is that investing is a powerful tool accessible to anyone who seeks financial growth and long-term wealth accumulation. By harnessing the power of compound interest and making informed investment decisions, individuals can grow their savings significantly and achieve their financial goals.

In this chapter, we will delve into the fundamentals of investing and see how you can make your money work for you. We will demystify the jargon, explain different investment vehicles, and guide you through the process of constructing an investment portfolio tailored to your goals and risk tolerance. Whether you are a complete beginner or looking to enhance your investment strategies, this chapter will equip you with the knowledge and confidence needed to navigate the world of investments.

10.1 The Power of Compound Interest in Wealth Accumulation

Investing is a powerful tool that can help you grow your wealth over time and achieve your financial goals. One key concept to understand when it comes to investing is the power of compound interest.

Compound interest is the process of earning interest on the initial amount of money you invest and any interest or returns your investment generates over time. This means that not only does your initial investment grow, but the growth itself also earns additional returns.

To illustrate the power of compound interest, let me give you an example. Imagine you invested $1,000 in an investment vehicle that earns an average annual return of 8%. At the end of the first year, your investment would grow to $1,080. However, in the second year, you wouldn't just earn 8% on your initial investment of $1,000; you would earn 8% on the new total of $1,080. This cycle continues year after year, resulting in exponential growth.

The impact of compound interest becomes truly remarkable over a long period of time. Let's say you invest $500 per month for 30 years with an average annual return of 7%. At the end of those 30 years, your investment would grow to nearly $900,000. This significant growth is primarily due to the power of compound interest.

Understanding compound interest lets you make informed

decisions about when and how much to invest. The earlier you start investing, the longer your money has to benefit from compound interest. Even small amounts invested regularly can accumulate into substantial sums over time.

However, it's important to remember that investing always carries risks. The value of investments can go up or down, and factors such as inflation and market fluctuations can impact your returns. That's why it's crucial to educate yourself about different investment options, diversify your portfolio to manage risk, and seek professional advice if needed.

By harnessing the power of compound interest and making smart investment choices, you can set yourself up for long-term financial growth and create a secure future for yourself and your loved ones.

Remember, investing is not a get-rich-quick scheme but a disciplined approach to wealth accumulation over time. By staying focused on your long-term goals and being patient through market ups and downs, you can reap the rewards of compounding and achieve financial independence.

10.2 Risk Tolerance Assessment and Investment Objectives

Risk tolerance refers to an individual's willingness and ability to withstand fluctuations in their investment portfolio. Being aware of your risk tolerance is crucial as it will determine the types of investments you should consider. Some people have a high tolerance for risk and are comfortable with investments that have the potential for significant returns and higher volatility. Others have a lower risk tolerance and prefer more stable investments with lower potential returns.

To assess your risk tolerance, consider factors such as your financial goals, time horizon, income stability, and emotional response to market fluctuations. Additionally, understanding your beliefs about money and your ability to handle financial setbacks can provide valuable insights into your risk tolerance.

Once you have determined your risk tolerance, it is important to establish clear investment objectives. These objectives will serve as a roadmap for your investment strategy and help you stay focused on your long-term financial goals. Here are some common investment objectives to consider.

Capital Preservation: If your primary goal is to preserve your initial investment, you may opt for lower-risk investments such as bonds or money market funds. These investments typically provide steady income with minimal risk.

Income Generation: If you are looking to generate regular income from your investments, consider dividend-paying stocks, real estate investment trusts (REITs), or bond funds. These types of investments can provide reliable income streams.

Growth: If you have a longer time horizon and are willing to take on more risk, growth-oriented investments such as individual stocks or exchange-traded funds (ETFs) may be suitable. These investments have the potential for higher returns but also come with greater volatility.

Diversification: Another objective to consider is diversification, which involves spreading your investments across different asset classes (e.g., stocks, bonds, real estate). Diversification helps reduce risk by minimizing the impact of any single investment's performance on your overall portfolio.

Socially Responsible Investing: If investing in companies that align with your values is important to you, consider socially responsible investing (SRI). SRI focuses on supporting businesses that prioritize environmental sustainability, social justice, or corporate governance.

When setting investment objectives, it is crucial to ensure they align with your overall financial goals and risk tolerance. Keep in mind that investment objectives may change over time as your circumstances evolve.

10.3 Diversification Strategies to Minimize Risk

Diversification is a key concept in investment that allows you to spread your risk across different asset classes and investments. By diversifying your portfolio, you can reduce the impact of any single investment's performance on your overall financial health.

One common diversification strategy is to invest in a mix of stocks, bonds, and other assets. This approach is known as asset allocation, and it involves dividing your investment portfolio into different asset classes based on your risk tolerance and investment goals. By investing in a variety of assets, you can reduce the potential negative impact of any one asset class underperforming.

For example, let's say you have $10,000 to invest. Instead of putting all of your money into one stock, you could allocate a portion to stocks, another portion to bonds, and another portion to cash or other investments. The specific allocation will depend on your risk tolerance and investment objectives. By diversifying your investments across different asset classes, you can potentially minimize the impact of market fluctuations on your overall portfolio.

Another diversification strategy is to invest in different sectors or industries. Different sectors tend to perform differently based on various factors such as economic conditions, government regulations, technological advancements, and consumer trends. By spreading your investments across various sectors, you can reduce the risk of being heavily exposed to the performance of just one industry.

For instance, if you invest solely in the technology sector and there is a downturn in the tech industry, your entire portfolio may suffer significant losses. However, if you have diversified your investments across sectors such as healthcare, finance, energy, and retail, the negative impact of a downturn in one sector may be offset by the positive performance of other sectors.

Additionally, geographic diversification is another effective strategy for reducing investment risk. Investing solely in one country or region exposes you to risks specific to that location, such as political instability, economic downturns, or currency fluctuations. By expanding your investments globally, you can benefit from the potential growth opportunities offered by different economies while spreading the risk associated with any one country.

Moreover, investing in different types of financial instruments within an asset class can provide further diversification. For example, within the bond market, you could invest in government bonds, corporate bonds, municipal bonds, or even bond funds. Each type of bond carries its own level of risk and return potential. By diversifying across these types of bonds, you can spread your risk and potentially achieve more stable returns.

It is important to note that diversification does not guarantee profits or protect against losses. It is merely a risk management technique that aims to reduce the impact of adverse market events on your investment portfolio. While diversification can help mitigate risk, it is crucial to conduct thorough research and seek professional advice when building a diversified portfolio.

10.4 Asset Allocation Based on Individual Goals and Time Horizons

Once you have established your investment objectives and determined your risk tolerance, developing an asset allocation strategy will be the next step in growing your wealth. Asset allocation refers to the distribution of your investments across different types of assets, such as stocks, bonds, mutual funds, and other financial instruments.

The purpose of asset allocation is to create a diversified portfolio that balances risk and return. By spreading your investments across various asset classes, you can potentially reduce the impact of volatility in any single investment and increase the chances of achieving consistent long-term growth.

When it comes to determining the optimal asset allocation for your personal goals and time horizons, there are several factors to consider. First and foremost, you need to assess your financial objectives. Are you investing for short-term goals, such as a down payment on a house or a vacation? Or are you planning for long-term goals like retirement or funding your children's education?

The time horizon also plays a crucial role in determining asset allocation. Generally, the longer your investment time horizon, the more risk you can afford to take on. This is because you have more time to recover from any short-term market downturns. On the other hand, if you have a shorter time horizon, such as less than five years, it is advisable to focus on more conservative investments with lower volatility.

129

Another factor to consider is your risk tolerance. Some individuals may be comfortable with higher levels of risk in pursuit of potentially higher returns, while others prefer a more conservative approach to protect their capital. It is important to understand your own comfort level with risk and make investment decisions accordingly.

A commonly used framework for asset allocation is the rule of thumb called the "100 minus age" rule. According to this rule, subtract your age from 100 to determine the percentage of your portfolio that should be allocated to stocks. The remaining percentage can be allocated to bonds or other fixed-income investments. For example, if you are 30 years old, you could allocate 70% of your portfolio to stocks and 30% to bonds.

However, it's worth noting that this rule is a guideline and not a one-size-fits-all approach. When determining the right asset allocation for you, it's important to consider your specific financial situation, goals, risk tolerance, and market conditions.

In addition to stocks and bonds, you may consider diversifying your portfolio further by including alternative investments such as real estate, commodities, or even cryptocurrencies. These alternative investments can provide additional diversification benefits and potential opportunities for growth.

10.5 Understanding Investment Vehicles

When it comes to investing, understanding the different types of investment vehicles is crucial. These vehicles act as tools through which you can grow your wealth over time. Let's take a look at some of the most common investment options for beginners.

Stocks: Stocks represent ownership shares in a company. When you buy stocks, you become a shareholder and have the potential to earn returns through dividends and capital appreciation. Stocks offer the opportunity for higher returns but also come with higher risks.

Bonds: Bonds are debt securities issued by governments, municipalities, and corporations to raise capital. When you invest in bonds, you are essentially lending money to the issuer in exchange for periodic interest payments and the return of the principal amount at maturity. Bonds are generally considered less risky than stocks but offer lower potential returns.

Mutual Funds: Mutual funds pool money from multiple investors and invest in a diversified portfolio of stocks, bonds, or other assets. They are managed by professional fund managers who make investment decisions on behalf of the investors. Mutual funds offer instant diversification and are suitable for those who prefer a hands-off approach to investing.

Exchange-Traded Funds (ETFs): ETFs are similar to mutual funds but trade on stock exchanges like individual stocks. They offer diversification and liquidity while often having lower expense ratios compared to mutual funds. ETFs can track specific indexes or sectors, providing investors with exposure to a wide range of assets.

Real Estate Investment Trusts (REITs): REITs allow individuals to invest in real estate without directly purchasing properties. These trusts own and manage income-generating properties such as office buildings, apartments, hotels, or shopping centers. Investing in REITs can provide regular income through dividends and potential capital appreciation.

Index Funds: Index funds aim to replicate the performance of a specific market index, such as the S&P 500 or the Dow Jones Industrial Average. By investing in index funds, you can gain exposure to a broad range of stocks or bonds at a relatively low cost. Index funds are known for their passive management approach and generally have lower expense ratios compared to actively managed funds.

Certificates of Deposit (CDs): CDs are time deposits offered by banks and credit unions. They have fixed terms ranging from a few months to several years and offer a fixed interest rate during that period. CDs are considered safe investments as they are insured by the Federal Deposit Insurance Corporation (FDIC) up to certain limits.

Money Market Accounts: Money market accounts are savings accounts that typically offer higher interest rates than regular savings accounts. They provide easy access to your money while still earning interest. Money market accounts often come with limited check-writing privileges and require higher minimum balances compared to regular savings accounts.

Commodities: Commodities include physical goods such as gold, silver, oil, natural gas, agricultural products, etc. They can be invested in through various methods, including futures contracts and exchange-traded commodities (ETCs). Investing in commodities can provide diversification benefits and potential protection against inflation.

Cryptocurrencies: Cryptocurrencies like Bitcoin and Ethereum have gained popularity in recent years. These digital currencies operate on decentralized networks using blockchain technology. Cryptocurrencies carry high volatility and risk but can potentially have significant returns.

By understanding these different investment vehicles, you can make informed decisions about which ones align with your financial goals, risk tolerance, and time horizon. Remember that diversification is key to managing risk and maximizing returns in your investment portfolio.

Before making any investment decisions, research each option thoroughly, considering factors such as historical performance, fees, management expertise, and market conditions. Also, consult with a financial advisor or investment professional who can provide personalized guidance based on your financial situation.

With a solid understanding of these investment vehicles, you will be better equipped to begin building wealth and achieving your financial goals over time.

10.6 Tools for Evaluating Investment Opportunities and Monitoring Performance

Investing in various financial instruments can be a daunting prospect, especially for beginners. However, with the right tools and knowledge, you can make informed decisions and grow your wealth over time.

Financial News Platforms: Staying updated with the latest financial news is crucial for making well-informed investment decisions. Platforms such as Bloomberg, CNBC, and Financial Times provide comprehensive coverage of market trends, economic indicators, and company news. Understanding the broader economic landscape allows you to identify potential investment opportunities and assess their viability.

Stock Screeners: Stock screeners are powerful tools that allow you to filter stocks based on specific criteria. These criteria could include factors like market capitalization, industry sector, dividend yield, price-to-earnings ratio, and more. By using stock screeners like Yahoo Finance, you can narrow down your options and focus on companies that meet your investment objectives.

Fundamental Analysis Tools: Fundamental analysis involves evaluating a company's financial health by examining its financial statements, earnings reports, and other key metrics. Tools such as Morningstar, Yahoo Finance, and Google Finance provide access to these financial documents and allow you to analyze important ratios like return on equity, debt-to-equity ratio, and earnings per share. By conducting a thorough fundamental analysis, you can gain insights into a company's performance and make informed investment decisions.

Technical Analysis Software: Technical analysis involves studying charts and patterns to predict future price movements of stocks or other financial instruments. Software like TradingView or MetaTrader provides advanced charting tools that enable you to analyze price trends, moving averages, support and resistance levels, and various technical indicators. Using these tools, you can identify your investments' potential entry or exit points.

Portfolio Tracking Apps: Tracking your investments is essential for monitoring their performance and assessing their overall impact on your financial goals. Portfolio tracking apps like Personal Capital or Mint allow you to consolidate all your investments in one place and provide real-time updates on their performance. These apps often offer features like asset allocation analysis, investment fee tracking, and goal tracking to help you stay on top of your investments.

Investment Calculators: Investment calculators are invaluable when it comes to projecting future returns or evaluating the impact of certain variables on your investments. Tools like Bankrate's investment calculator or Vanguard's retirement calculator allow you to input various parameters such as initial investment amount, expected rate of return, and time horizon to estimate the growth of your investments over time. Using these calculators lets you make more informed decisions regarding your investment strategies.

10.7 Wrapping It Up

In this chapter, we have delved into the world of investing and explored how it can contribute to growing wealth over time. We discussed the power of compound interest and how it plays a significant role in accumulating wealth. We can make informed decisions about asset allocation and diversification strategies by assessing our risk tolerance and investment objectives.

Understanding various investment vehicles such as stocks, bonds, and mutual funds is crucial in making sound investment choices. We also learned about tools for evaluating investment opportunities and monitoring performance to ensure we are on track toward our financial goals.

As we conclude this chapter, it is important to emphasize that investing is a long-term endeavor. It requires patience, discipline, and continuous learning. Market fluctuations and economic trends will always be a part of the investment land-scape, but by staying informed and adapting our strategies accordingly, we can navigate through them.

Investing involves risks, and it's essential to seek advice from qualified professionals before making any major investment decisions. Everyone's financial situation and goals are unique, so we must tailor our investment strategies accordingly.

By incorporating investing into our overall financial plan, we can enhance our financial growth potential and work towards building wealth for the future. Investing is an opportunity to create passive income streams and achieve financial freedom.

As you move forward on your personal finance journey, continue to educate yourself about investing trends, seek new opportunities, and review your investment portfolio regularly. Doing so allows you to make adjustments as needed and stay on track toward your financial goals.

In the next chapter, we will explore another avenue for wealth building: real estate.

Chapter 11: Real Estate Wealth Building

"The best investment on earth is earth." – *Louis Glickman*

Real estate has long been recognized as a powerful asset class for building wealth. From residential properties to commercial developments, real estate allows individuals to generate passive income, achieve long-term appreciation, and diversify their investment portfolios. But how exactly can beginners navigate the complex world of real estate investing?

In this chapter, we will delve into the intricacies of real estate wealth building and provide a comprehensive guide to help you make informed decisions in this exciting field. Whether you aspire to become a landlord, invest in REITs (Real Estate Investment Trusts), or flip properties for profit, understanding the fundamental principles and strategies is essential.

We will begin by exploring the various types of properties, locations, and market trends that you need to consider before making any investment decisions. You will learn how to evaluate potential returns and analyze the risks of different real estate ventures. Additionally, we will discuss financing options available to real estate investors and provide insights into property management considerations for those who choose to be more hands-on with their investments.

Throughout this chapter, we will emphasize the importance of thorough research and due diligence while also highlighting the potential rewards that come with smart real estate investments. We will share practical tips, case studies, and real-life examples to illustrate key concepts, enabling you to develop a solid foundation of knowledge in this dynamic field.

Remember, real estate can be a powerful tool for wealth creation, but it requires careful planning, risk management, and ongoing education. By mastering the principles outlined in this chapter, you will be equipped with the essential skills to navigate the complex world of real estate wealth building.

11.1 Exploring Real Estate as an Investment Option

Real estate has long been considered a popular and lucrative investment option for individuals looking to build wealth over time. Whether it's residential properties, commercial buildings, or even raw land, the real estate market offers numerous opportunities for investors to grow their financial portfolios.

When exploring real estate as an investment option, it's important to understand the various factors that come into play.

One key consideration when investing in real estate is understanding the different types of properties available and the potential advantages they offer. Residential properties, such as single-family homes, townhouses, or condominiums, can provide a stable source of rental income and potential long-term appreciation. On the other hand, commercial properties, including office spaces, retail buildings, or industrial warehouses, offer higher potential returns but often require a larger initial investment.

Location is another critical factor to consider when investing in real estate. The value of a property is greatly influenced by its proximity to essential amenities, transportation hubs, schools, and employment opportunities. Understanding local market trends and analyzing the potential for growth in a specific area can help you identify profitable investment opportunities.

Financing options also play a significant role in real estate investments. Understanding different financing strategies, such as traditional mortgages, private lenders, or partnerships, can help you determine the best approach for your investment goals. Evaluating interest rates, loan terms, and repayment options is crucial to ensure your investment remains financially viable.

Analyzing potential returns on real estate investments involves assessing both short-term cash flow and long-term appreciation. To determine profitability, rental income from tenants and property management costs should be carefully considered. Additionally, studying market trends and historical data can provide insights into the potential appreciation of your investment over time.

Property management considerations are also important for real estate investors. Whether to manage the property yourself or hire professional property managers depends on your availability and expertise. Effective property management ensures optimal tenant occupancy rates, regular maintenance and repairs, and timely rent collections.

As you delve into real estate investing, it's essential to develop long-term strategies that align with your financial goals. This may involve diversifying your portfolio by acquiring properties in different locations or exploring alternative strategies such as fix-and-flip or buy-and-hold investments.

Real estate investing offers unique advantages such as tax benefits and leverage—the ability to control a large asset with a relatively small down payment. Understanding these advantages and how they can work in your favor is crucial for maximizing returns while mitigating risks.

11.2 Understanding Property Types, Locations, and Market Trends

When it comes to real estate investment, one key factor to consider is understanding property types, locations, and market trends. This knowledge will help you make informed decisions and maximize your potential returns.

Property Types

Before diving into real estate investment, it's important to familiarize yourself with the different types of properties available:

- Residential Properties: These include single-family homes, condominiums, townhouses, and apartment buildings. Residential properties are often considered a safe and stable investment option.
- Commercial Properties: This category includes office buildings, retail spaces, industrial warehouses, and mixed-use buildings. Investing in commercial properties can offer higher potential returns but carries additional risks.
- Rental Properties: Owning rental properties allows you to generate income by leasing to tenants. This can be a lucrative long-term investment strategy if managed properly.
- Vacation Properties: Buying a vacation property can provide personal enjoyment and potential rental income when not used. However, it's crucial to thoroughly research the location's tourism industry and property management options before making a purchase.

Location Analysis

The saying "location, location, location" holds true in real estate investing. The location of a property greatly influences its desirability and potential for appreciation. Here are some key factors to consider when analyzing the location:

- Economic Growth: Look for areas with strong economic indicators such as job growth, population increase, and vibrant industries. These factors contribute to a healthy real estate market.

- Infrastructure: Assess the quality of infrastructure in the area, including transportation networks, schools, healthcare facilities, and amenities. Good infrastructure can attract tenants or buyers and drive property value.
- Neighborhood Dynamics: Study the neighborhood's demographics, crime rates, school districts, and proximity to amenities like parks, shopping centers, and entertainment venues. A desirable neighborhood enhances property value and demand.
- Future Development Plans: Research any planned or ongoing development projects in the area. New infrastructure or commercial developments can significantly impact property values.
- Market Saturation: Analyze supply and demand dynamics within the local housing market. If there is an oversupply of properties or declining demand, it may indicate a less favorable investment opportunity.

Market Trends

Staying updated on real estate market trends is essential for successful investing. Here are some key trends to watch out for:

- Price Appreciation: Monitor historical price trends in the area to assess the potential for future appreciation. Look for signs of steady growth or turnaround in previously undervalued neighborhoods.
- Rental Rates: Analyze rental rates in the local market to determine the income potential of a rental property.

Consider factors such as vacancy rates, rental demand, and average rental yields.

- Mortgage Rates: Keep an eye on mortgage interest rates as they directly impact affordability for both buyers and investors. Lower rates can incentivize buying activity and drive up property prices.
- Regulatory Changes: Stay informed about any changes in real estate regulations that may affect your investment strategies. Changes to tax laws or zoning regulations can have significant implications for your investments.

11.3 Financing Options for Real Estate Investments

When it comes to investing in real estate, one of the most crucial considerations is determining how you will finance your investments. There are several financing options available, each with its own advantages and considerations.

Traditional Mortgage Loans: This is perhaps the most popular and widely used financing option for real estate investments. With a traditional mortgage loan, you borrow money from a lender to purchase a property and then repay the loan over a set period of time with interest. The terms and conditions of mortgage loans can vary, so it's important to shop around and compare different lenders to find the best rates and terms that suit your needs. Remember that traditional mortgage loans typically require a down payment, usually ranging from 5% to 20% of the property's value.

Hard Money Loans: Unlike traditional mortgage loans, hard money loans are often provided by private investors or companies. These loans are typically short-term and have higher interest rates compared to traditional mortgages. Hard money loans are commonly used by real estate investors who need quick access to funding or cannot qualify for traditional financing due to credit or income limitations. It's important to consider the terms and costs of hard money loans before proceeding, as they can be riskier than other financing options.

Private Money Loans: Like hard money loans, private money loans involve borrowing funds from individuals or private lenders rather than traditional financial institutions. Private money loans can offer more flexibility in terms of loan terms and requirements, as they are often based on personal relationships or connections within the real estate investing community. When opting for private money loans, it's essential to establish clear terms and expectations with the lender to ensure a mutually beneficial arrangement.

Seller Financing: In some cases, sellers may be willing to finance a portion or all of the purchase price of a property instead of requiring traditional financing. With seller financing, you make regular payments directly to the seller over an agreed-upon timeframe, eliminating the need for a mortgage lender. This option can be particularly beneficial if you cannot secure a conventional loan or want more negotiating power in the transaction. However, it's important to conduct thorough due diligence and ensure that the terms of the seller financing arrangement align with your financial goals.

Partnership Financing: Another option for financing real estate investments is partnering with other investors or individuals who can provide capital for the acquisition of properties. This can be an effective way to pool financial resources and share both risks and rewards. When entering into a partnership agreement, it's crucial to outline roles, responsibilities, profit-sharing arrangements, and exit strategies to avoid potential conflicts down the line.

Crowdfunding: With the advent of technology, crowdfunding platforms have emerged as an alternative source of funding for real estate investments. These platforms allow individual investors to contribute small amounts of money towards specific real estate projects in exchange for a proportional ownership stake or return on investment. Crowdfunding can provide access to diverse investment opportunities with potentially lower entry requirements. However, it's important to thoroughly research crowdfunding platforms and carefully evaluate the risks associated with each project before investing.

When choosing a financing option for your real estate investments, consider factors such as your financial situation, risk tolerance, objectives, and timeline. It's advisable to consult with a financial advisor or mortgage professional who specializes in real estate investing to help you navigate these options and make informed decisions.

11.4 Analyzing Potential Returns on Real Estate Investments

When it comes to building wealth through real estate, one of the most important aspects to consider is the potential returns on your investments. Understanding how to analyze these returns will help you make informed decisions and maximize your financial gains.

To begin, let's take a look at some key factors that can impact the returns on real estate investments:

Rental Income: One of the primary sources of returns from real estate investments is rental income. This is the income generated from tenants who pay to live or operate their businesses in your property. Analyzing the rental income potential involves considering factors such as location, demand for rental properties in the area, and rental rates comparable to similar properties.

Cash Flow: Cash flow is an essential component of real estate investing and refers to the amount of money left over after deducting expenses (such as mortgage payments, property taxes, insurance, and maintenance costs) from rental income. Positive cash flow indicates that your investment is generating a surplus income, while negative cash flow means you are spending more than you are earning from the property.

Appreciation: Real estate properties have the potential to appreciate in value over time, which can contribute significantly to your overall returns. Appreciation is influenced by various factors such as location, market conditions, infrastructure developments, and economic growth in the area. Analyzing historical trends and future projections can provide insights into a property's expected appreciation potential.

Tax Benefits: Real estate investments often come with various tax benefits that can further enhance your returns. These may include deductions for mortgage interest, property taxes, depreciation expenses, and even tax deferral strategies through 1031 exchanges. Understanding the tax implications and leveraging these benefits can have a positive impact on your overall returns.

Leverage: Real estate investments offer unique opportunities for leveraging borrowed funds to acquire properties. By using leverage, you can control a larger asset with less initial capital investment. However, it's essential to carefully manage the risks associated with leverage and ensure that the potential returns outweigh the costs of borrowing.

Now that we have identified these key factors, let's discuss how to analyze the potential returns on a real estate investment.

Cash-on-Cash Return: This metric calculates the annual return on your actual cash investment in a property. It considers factors such as rental income, expenses, and any financing costs associated with the investment. A higher cash-on-cash return indicates a more favorable investment opportunity.

Cap Rate (Capitalization Rate): The cap rate is calculated by dividing a property's Net Operating Income (NOI) by its purchase price or appraised value. It provides an estimate of the property's potential return on investment based solely on its income-generating capabilities. A higher cap rate suggests a higher potential return.

Return on Investment (ROI): ROI measures the profitability of an investment relative to its cost. It considers both cash flows (rental income minus expenses) and any appreciation gained over a specific period. ROI helps determine whether an investment is meeting your financial goals and expectations.

Internal Rate of Return (IRR): IRR is a more comprehensive measure that considers both cash flows and the time value of money. It represents the annualized percentage rate at which an investment breaks even or generates a specified return. You can evaluate whether a real estate investment is worthwhile by comparing the IRR to alternative investments or industry benchmarks.

Sensitivity Analysis: It's crucial to conduct a sensitivity analysis on your real estate investment to assess its performance under different scenarios or assumptions. For example, you may want to determine how changes in vacancy rates, rental prices, or interest rates would affect your expected returns.

By thoroughly analyzing these metrics and conducting due diligence on potential real estate investments, you can make informed decisions and increase your chances of achieving favorable returns. Remember that investing in real estate involves inherent risks, and it's crucial to seek professional advice or consult experienced investors to mitigate these risks.

11.5 Property Management Considerations for Real Estate Investors

Investing in real estate can be a lucrative way to build wealth and secure financial stability. However, successful real estate investing requires more than just acquiring properties. It also involves effective property management to maximize returns and minimize risks.

Property management is the process of overseeing and maintaining real estate investments. Whether you choose to manage your properties yourself or hire a professional property manager, there are several key considerations to keep in mind.

Tenant Screening: Finding reliable and responsible tenants is crucial for successful property management. Conduct thorough background checks, verify employment and income, and check references to ensure you choose tenants who are likely to pay their rent on time and take care of the property.

Lease Agreements: Establish clear and comprehensive lease agreements that outline tenant responsibilities, rent payment terms, and rules and regulations for the property. A well-drafted lease agreement can help avoid misunderstandings and conflicts with tenants.

Rent Collection: Implement an efficient system for collecting rent from tenants. This may include setting up online payment options and clearly communicating rent due dates and consequences for late payments. Consistent and timely rent collection is essential for maintaining positive cash flow.

Property Maintenance: Regular maintenance and repairs are necessary to keep your property in good condition and attract quality tenants. Create a schedule for routine maintenance tasks such as landscaping, cleaning, and inspections. Promptly address any repair issues reported by tenants to prevent further damage.

Property Insurances: Protect your investment by obtaining appropriate insurance coverage for your rental property. This may include landlord insurance or a specialized rental dwelling policy. Insurance can provide financial protection against potential damages, liability claims, or loss of rental income.

Tenant Relations: Building positive relationships with your tenants can lead to longer tenancies and greater tenant satisfaction. Respond promptly to tenant inquiries or concerns, maintain open lines of communication, and address any issues that arise in a fair and respectful manner.

Compliance with Legal Requirements: Familiarize yourself with local landlord-tenant laws and regulations to ensure compliance. Stay informed about changes in legislation that may affect rental property owners, such as rent control laws, eviction procedures, and safety requirements.

Financial Management: Maintain accurate records of income and expenses related to your rental properties. Keep track of rental income, mortgage payments, property taxes, insurance premiums, maintenance costs, and other expenses associated with property management. This will make tax filing easier and provide insights into the financial performance of your investments.

Eviction Procedures: In cases where tenants fail to meet their contractual obligations or violate lease terms, eviction proceedings may be necessary. Familiarize yourself with the legal steps required for eviction in your jurisdiction and follow the proper procedures to protect your rights as a landlord.

Ongoing Education: Stay updated on industry trends, best practices, and new laws or regulations affecting property management through continuing education initiatives or professional associations. Networking with other real estate investors can also provide valuable insights and resources.

Effective property management is vital for long-term success in real estate investing. By ensuring professional tenant screening, implementing comprehensive lease agreements, maintaining properties, building positive tenant relations, complying with legal requirements, managing finances diligently, understanding eviction procedures when needed, and staying educated about industry trends, you can confidently navigate the challenges of property management.

11.6 Long-term Strategies for Building Wealth through Real Estate

Real estate has long been considered a lucrative investment option for those looking to build wealth over time. While it may require a significant upfront investment, the potential returns and benefits can be well worth it in the long run.

One of the most effective long-term strategies for building wealth through real estate is property appreciation. Over time, properties in desirable locations tend to increase in value, allowing you to generate significant returns on your initial investment. By carefully selecting properties in areas with high potential for growth and development, you can benefit from capital appreciation as the market improves.

Another strategy for building wealth through real estate is rental income. Purchasing properties and renting them out can provide you with a steady stream of passive income, which can be reinvested or used to cover expenses. Rental income can grow over time as you increase rents in line with market rates and pay down your mortgage, resulting in higher cash flow and improved profitability.

To maximize your rental income, you should select properties that have a strong rental demand and are located in areas with favorable rental market conditions. Conduct thorough research on rental rates in the area, vacancy rates, and tenant demographics to ensure that your property will attract reliable tenants and generate consistent cash flow.

Property flipping is another popular strategy for building wealth through real estate. This involves purchasing properties at below-market prices, renovating or improving them, and then selling them at a profit. Successful property flipping requires a keen eye for finding undervalued properties, understanding renovation costs and potential returns, and timing the sale to maximize profits.

Investing in real estate investment trusts (REITs) or real estate mutual funds is another way to build wealth through real estate without directly owning properties. REITs pool funds from multiple investors to invest in income-generating properties such as commercial buildings, apartments, or shopping centers. By investing in REITs, you can benefit from rental income and property appreciation without the hassle of property management.

It's important to note that building wealth through real estate requires careful planning, research, and a long-term perspective. Real estate investments are not without risks, and market conditions can fluctuate over time. It's essential to diversify your real estate portfolio by investing in different types of properties across various locations to mitigate risk and maximize returns.

Additionally, maintaining good relationships with professionals such as real estate agents, property managers, and contractors can greatly enhance your chances of success in the real estate market. These individuals can provide valuable insights, advice, and support throughout your real estate investment journey.

Real estate offers numerous opportunities for building wealth over time. Whether it's through property appreciation, rental income, property flipping, or investing in REITs, there are various strategies you can employ to maximize your financial gains. However, it's crucial to approach real estate investment cautiously, conduct thorough research, and seek professional guidance when needed. With a long-term perspective and careful planning, real estate can be an excellent avenue for building wealth and securing your financial future.

11.7 Wrapping It Up

In this chapter, we delved into the world of real estate as an investment option. We explored the strategies for building wealth through property ownership. We discussed various aspects, such as understanding property types, locations, market trends, financing options, analyzing potential returns, and property management considerations. We also discussed long-term strategies for sustainable wealth-building in the real estate market.

Real estate has long been recognized as a lucrative investment avenue, providing individuals with opportunities to grow their wealth over time. Investing in properties strategically allows you to leverage the power of appreciation and rental income to create a secure financial future for yourself.

However, it is essential to approach real estate investment with caution and a thorough understanding of the market dynamics. Before making any investment decisions, make sure to conduct extensive research, consult professionals if needed, and carefully evaluate the potential risks and rewards associated with each property.

Remember that real estate investments require a long-term commitment. Patience and a forward-thinking mindset are crucial when it comes to property ownership. While real estate can offer substantial returns, it is important to recognize that it may take time for your investments to mature and yield significant profits.

As you embark on your journey towards building wealth through real estate, remember that this chapter serves as an introduction to the topic. There is always more to learn and explore as you gain experience in the field. Stay curious, stay informed, and continuously adapt your strategies based on changing market conditions and personal goals.

In the next chapter, we will shift our focus to retirement planning, a critical aspect of securing your financial future.

Chapter 12: Retirement Planning

"Retirement is not the end of the road; it is the beginning of the open highway leading to unlimited possibilities."

As we journey through life, it is essential to plan for our future, and retirement planning is a crucial aspect of that journey. Retirement may seem far off when we are young, but it is never too early to start considering securing our financial well-being for the golden years. In this chapter, we will delve into the intricacies of retirement planning and explore strategies to help you achieve a comfortable and fulfilling retirement.

Retirement planning is not just about setting aside money; it involves careful consideration of your desired lifestyle and calculating how much you will need to support that lifestyle during your retirement years. It requires understanding the various retirement savings accounts available, such as Individual Retirement Accounts (IRA), 401(k) plans, and pensions. Additionally, maximizing contributions to retirement accounts and taking advantage of employer matches can significantly impact your ability to build a substantial nest egg.

While retirement planning may seem daunting, it is a critical endeavor that can provide peace of mind and financial security in your later years. Whether you dream of traveling the world or spending quality time with loved ones, a well-thought-out retirement plan can help turn those dreams into reality.

In this chapter, we will guide you through each step of the retirement planning process. We will explore how to establish clear retirement goals based on your desired lifestyle and calculate your retirement needs accordingly. We will also discuss the different types of retirement savings accounts and provide strategies for maximizing contributions while taking advantage of employer matches and incentives.

Transitioning from the accumulation phase to the distribution phase in retirement planning requires careful consideration of managing your nest egg effectively. We will offer insights into managing your investments wisely during retirement to ensure a sustainable income stream. Additionally, we will delve into long-term strategies for maintaining a comfortable retirement and adapting your financial plan as circumstances change.

Retirement should be a time of joy and relaxation, where you can reap the rewards of your hard work and enjoy the fruits of your labor. By taking control of your financial future through comprehensive retirement planning, you can secure the life you envision after your working years.

12.1 Establishing Retirement Goals Based on Desired Lifestyle

Retirement is a significant milestone in life, and it is essential to plan for it to secure your future and maintain financial stability. The first step in this journey is to establish retirement goals based on your desired lifestyle.

Retirement goals are deeply personal and can vary from person to person. Some individuals may aspire to travel the world, while others may prefer a quieter life close to home. Take some time to envision your ideal retirement – the activities you want to engage in, the places you want to visit, and the level of financial security you desire.

Once you have a clear vision, it's time to put your goals into perspective. Consider factors such as your current age, anticipated retirement age, and life expectancy. These factors will help you determine how many years you need to save and how much money you'll require during retirement.

It is crucial to be realistic about your retirement goals. While it's wonderful to dream big, it's also important to ensure that your goals are achievable within your financial means. Consider your current income, expenses, and savings potential when setting these goals.

Additionally, consider potential sources of income during retirement. Will you rely solely on your retirement savings, or do you have other sources, such as pensions or rental income? Factoring in these additional income streams will give you a more accurate picture of what you need to save.

12.2 Calculating Retirement Needs Based on Anticipated Expenses

As you plan for your retirement, it is crucial to calculate your anticipated expenses to ensure that you have enough savings to support your desired lifestyle. Retirement is when you should be able to enjoy the fruits of your labor and live comfortably without financial stress. To determine your retirement needs, you must consider several factors impacting your expenses during this phase of life.

One of the first considerations when calculating retirement needs is estimating basic living expenses. These include essential costs such as housing, food, utilities, transportation, and healthcare. Start by examining your current budget and making adjustments for any foreseeable changes in these expenses. For example, you may have paid off your mortgage by the time you retire, which could reduce your housing costs. On the other hand, healthcare expenses tend to increase as we age, so it's essential to account for potential medical costs.

In addition to basic living expenses, think about the activities and experiences you envision enjoying during retirement. Do you plan to travel extensively or pursue expensive hobbies? Factor in these discretionary expenses when determining your retirement needs. It's important to strike a balance between enjoying your retirement and ensuring that your savings can sustain you throughout your golden years.

Another factor to consider is inflation. Over time, the pur-chasing power of money decreases due to inflation. Therefore, it is crucial to account for inflation when calculating your retirement needs. Generally, financial experts recommend assuming an average annual inflation rate of 2-3% when projecting future expenses. By factoring in inflation, you can ensure that your savings grow at a rate that keeps pace with rising prices.

Life expectancy is another critical factor to consider when estimating retirement needs. With advancements in healthcare and increased longevity, people are living longer than ever before. Planning for a longer retirement period is important to avoid running out of money in your later years. Consider your family history and personal health habits, and consult with financial professionals who can provide insights into average life expectancy trends.

Calculating retirement needs involves making assumptions and projections about various aspects of your future lifestyle and finances. While it may feel overwhelming, it is a crucial step in ensuring that you have enough funds to support yourself during retirement. Working with a financial advisor can provide valuable guidance in estimating your retirement needs based on your unique circumstances.

Once you have estimated your retirement needs, compare them with your current savings and investments. This analysis will help you determine if you are on track or if adjustments need to be made. Suppose you find a shortfall between your estimated needs and existing savings. In that case, you may need to explore options such as increasing your contributions to retirement accounts or working longer to build up additional savings.

12.3 Evaluating Different Retirement Savings Accounts

As you embark on your journey toward retirement, it's crucial to explore and evaluate the different retirement savings accounts available to you. Understanding the options and making informed decisions can maximize your savings and ensure a comfortable future.

One popular retirement savings account is the Individual Retirement Account (IRA). There are two main types of IRAs: traditional and Roth. A traditional IRA allows you to contribute pre-tax income, meaning you won't pay taxes on the money until you withdraw it during retirement. Contributions to a traditional IRA may be tax-deductible, providing potential tax advantages in the present.

On the other hand, a Roth IRA offers a different approach. Contributions to a Roth IRA are made with after-tax income, meaning you won't have to pay taxes on withdrawals during retirement. This can be advantageous if you anticipate being in a higher tax bracket when you retire.

Another popular retirement savings account is the 401(k), which is typically offered by employers. With a 401(k), you have the opportunity to contribute a portion of your salary directly from your paycheck before taxes are taken out. Some employers even match a percentage of your contributions, effectively increasing your savings without any additional effort on your part.

One advantage of a 401(k) is that contributions are made automatically, making it easier to consistently save for retirement. Additionally, the contributions to a 401(k) are tax-deferred, meaning you won't pay taxes on them until withdrawal during retirement.

When evaluating these retirement savings accounts and others that may be available to you, consider factors such as contribution limits, tax implications, investment options, and withdrawal rules. Each account has its own unique features and benefits, so take the time to research and understand how they align with your financial goals.

It's also important to note that you are not limited to just one type of retirement account. In fact, many individuals diversify their savings by contributing to an IRA and a 401(k). This approach allows for flexibility and potentially enhances the benefits of each account.

12.4 Strategies for Maximizing Contributions and Taking Advantage of Employer Matches/Retirement Plans

Understanding your employer's retirement plan is one of the first steps toward maximizing contributions. Take the time to review the plan documents provided by your employer and familiarize yourself with the details. This includes learning about contribution limits, vesting schedules, and any matching contributions your employer may offer.

Once you understand your employer's plan, consider contributing at least enough to receive the maximum employer match. Employer matches are essentially free money that can significantly boost your retirement savings. For example, if your employer offers a 50% match on contributions up to 6% of your salary, ensure that you contribute at least 6% to take full advantage of this benefit.

To further maximize your contributions, aim to contribute the maximum allowable amount to retirement accounts such as 401(k)s or IRAs each year.

If you find it challenging to allocate a significant portion of your income towards retirement savings, consider gradually increasing your contributions over time. Start with a modest percentage and gradually increase it by one or two percentage points each year until you reach your desired contribution level. This approach allows you to adjust to lower take-home pay while still making progress toward your retirement goals.

Another strategy to maximize contributions is to explore catch-up contributions. These additional contributions are available to individuals aged 50 or older, allowing them to contribute above the standard limits. Catch-up contributions can provide a valuable opportunity to accelerate your savings in the years leading up to retirement.

Furthermore, consider diversifying your retirement savings across different account types. If your employer offers both Roth and Traditional options, take advantage of their respective benefits. Roth contributions are made with after-tax dollars but allow tax-free withdrawals in retirement, while Traditional contributions are made with pre-tax dollars but are taxed upon withdrawal. Diversifying your contributions can provide flexibility in managing taxes during retirement.

Last but not least, regularly review and update your retirement plan as needed. Reassess your financial situation, goals, and risk tolerance periodically to ensure your investment allocations align with your long-term objectives. Consult with a financial advisor to make informed decisions regarding asset allocation and investment options within your retirement accounts.

12.5 Transitioning from Accumulation Phase to Distribution Phase in Retirement Planning

As you approach retirement age, your financial focus shifts from accumulating wealth to distributing and managing your savings. Transitioning from the accumulation phase to the distribution phase requires careful planning and consideration to ensure a comfortable retirement.

During the accumulation phase, your primary goal is to save and invest as much as possible for your retirement years. You may have been contributing to retirement accounts such as Individual Retirement Accounts (IRAs) or 401(k)s, taking advantage of employer matches or retirement plans, and making informed investment decisions. As you near retirement, evaluating your savings and investment strategies to align them with your desired retirement lifestyle is crucial.

One essential step in transitioning to the distribution phase is calculating your retirement needs based on anticipated expenses. Consider your desired standard of living, healthcare expenses, travel plans, and any other retirement goals you have in mind. By estimating your future expenses, you can create a realistic budget that accounts for both basic necessities and discretionary spending.

Once you have a clear understanding of your retirement needs, you can evaluate different retirement savings accounts to determine which ones best suit your circumstances. Traditional IRAs and 401(k)s offer tax-deferred growth but require mandatory minimum distributions (RMDs) starting at age 72. Roth IRAs provide tax-free withdrawals in retirement but involve paying taxes on contributions upfront.

Maximizing contributions to these accounts before reaching the required minimum distribution age can help grow your savings further. Additionally, taking advantage of catch-up contributions—extra amounts allowed for those aged 50 and above—can boost your nest egg even more.

It's also wise to consider how to manage Social Security benefits during the distribution phase. You can start claiming benefits as early as age 62, but delaying until full retirement age (typically between 66 and 67) or even later can result in higher monthly payments. Understanding the implications of when and how to claim Social Security benefits can significantly impact your overall retirement income.

As you transition into the distribution phase, it's crucial to develop a withdrawal strategy that balances meeting your financial needs and ensuring your savings' longevity. The 4% Rule is a common guideline suggesting that withdrawing 4% of your initial retirement portfolio balance each year, adjusted for inflation, should provide a sustainable income over a 30-year period.

However, every individual's circumstances are unique, and factors such as market performance, inflation rates, and health-care costs can influence the ideal withdrawal rate for you. Consulting with a financial advisor specializing in retirement planning can help you create a customized distribution strategy based on your specific needs and goals.

In addition to managing your withdrawals, it's essential to stay vigilant about asset allocation during the distribution phase. Balancing risk and reward becomes paramount as you rely on your savings for income. Rebalancing your investment portfolio periodically can help ensure it remains aligned with your risk tolerance while allowing potential growth opportunities.

12.6 Long-term Strategies for a Comfortable Retirement

Planning for retirement is a crucial aspect of personal finance, as it ensures financial security and peace of mind during your golden years.

As you approach retirement, it's essential to reassess your financial goals and make adjustments to your savings and investment strategies. Here are some key considerations for planning a financially secure retirement.

Evaluate Your Retirement Goals: Start by envisioning your ideal retirement lifestyle. Consider factors such as travel, hobbies, healthcare expenses, and any other aspirations you may have. By estimating your future expenses, you can determine how much income you'll need during retirement.

Calculate Retirement Needs: Once you have an idea of your retirement goals, calculate the amount of money needed to sustain your desired lifestyle. Take into account factors like inflation and potential healthcare costs. By thoroughly assessing your financial situation, you can develop a realistic plan for achieving your retirement goals.

Explore Retirement Savings Accounts: Familiarize yourself with the various retirement savings accounts available, such as Individual Retirement Accounts (IRAs) and employer-sponsored plans like 401(k)s. Understand the eligibility requirements, contribution limits, and tax advantages associated with each type of account. Maximize your contributions to these accounts to take advantage of any employer matches or tax benefits.

Diversify Your Investments: As you near retirement age, it's wise to adjust your investment portfolio to reduce risk. Consider shifting a portion of your investments from higher-risk assets to more stable options like bonds or cash equivalents. Diversifying your portfolio can help protect your savings from market volatility while still allowing for potential growth over time.

Transition to Distribution Phase: When you retire, you'll enter the distribution phase, which involves drawing income from your retirement savings. Determine an appropriate withdrawal strategy that ensures regular income while preserving the longevity of your nest egg. Research strategies like systematic withdrawals or annuities that provide a steady stream of income throughout retirement.

Consider Long-Term Care Insurance: Long-term care expenses can significantly impact your retirement savings if you require professional assistance with daily activities later in life. Investigate long-term care insurance options to mitigate the financial burden of such services. Compare different policies and understand the coverage they offer before making a decision.

Seek Professional Guidance: Retirement planning can be complex, so consider consulting with a financial advisor who specializes in it. An experienced advisor can help you navigate the intricacies of investment options, optimize tax strategies, and ensure your retirement plan aligns with your long-term goals.

12.7 Wrapping It Up

In this chapter, we have explored the crucial topic of retirement planning and securing your future. By now, you should clearly understand the steps involved in setting up a comfortable retirement that aligns with your desired lifestyle. Let's take a moment to recap the key concepts covered in this chapter.

First and foremost, we discussed the importance of establishing retirement goals based on your individual circumstances and aspirations. Whether you envision a peaceful retirement by the beach or an active one filled with travel and adventure, having a clear vision will help guide your financial decisions.

Next, we delved into calculating your retirement needs by considering anticipated expenses. From daily living costs to healthcare expenses and hobbies, it is essential to estimate these expenditures accurately to ensure you have enough funds to support yourself throughout retirement.

Additionally, we explored different retirement savings accounts such as IRAs and 401(k)s. Understanding the advantages and limitations of each account type can help you make informed decisions about which ones are best suited for your financial goals.

One crucial aspect of maximizing your retirement savings is taking advantage of employer matches and retirement plans. We discussed strategies for maximizing contributions and making the most of these valuable benefits offered by your employer.

As you progress from the accumulation phase to the distribution phase in retirement planning, it becomes essential to adjust your investment strategies accordingly. We explored various investment options suitable for retirees, taking into account your risk tolerance and income requirements during this phase of life.

Lastly, we discussed long-term strategies for a comfortable retirement, emphasizing the importance of ongoing monitoring and adjustments as circumstances change. Retirement planning is not a one-time event but an ongoing process requiring periodic reviews and modifications.

By following the guidance in this chapter and applying the knowledge gained throughout this book, you are well on your way to securing a financially sound future. Remember, taking control of your financial destiny starts with taking action today.

In the next chapter, we will delve into an area that is often overlooked but plays a significant role in our financial well-being: taxes.

Chapter 13: Taxes Made Easy

"An investment in knowledge pays the best interest." – *Benjamin Franklin*

As you journey through the realm of personal finance, it is essential to equip yourself with the basic knowledge and understanding of taxes. Although often viewed as a complex and daunting subject, taxes play a crucial role in shaping our financial growth and stability. By optimizing our tax strategies, we can unlock opportunities for maximizing our income, reducing our tax burden, and ultimately accelerating our path toward financial success.

In this chapter, we will delve into the intricacies of taxation systems and explore various strategies to optimize your tax returns. From common deductions and credits to tax-advantaged accounts and proactive planning techniques, we will equip you with the tools needed to make informed decisions that align with your financial goals.

But why is it important to understand taxes? Beyond the mere act of compliance, an understanding of taxation empowers you to take control of your finances. By recognizing the deductions and exemptions available to you, you can minimize your taxable income, potentially leading to significant savings. Furthermore, staying informed about changes in tax laws ensures that you are prepared to navigate any potential impact on your finances.

Throughout this chapter, we will demystify the world of taxes by providing easy-to-understand explanations, practical examples, and step-by-step guidance. We will explore the theoretical concepts and real-life scenarios through case studies to illustrate how tax optimization strategies can be applied in different situations.

Understanding taxes is vital for your financial well-being, whether you are an employee, a business owner, or a self-employed individual. Adopting a proactive approach toward tax planning can optimize your financial growth, protect your assets, and make informed decisions that align with your long-term goals.

13.1 Understanding the Basics of Taxation Systems

Taxes play a crucial role in personal finance, and understanding the basics of taxation systems is essential for financial growth.

Taxes are an integral part of our society, supporting public services and infrastructure that benefit us all. However, navigating the intricacies of tax laws can be overwhelming. By breaking down the basics, we aim to empower you to make informed decisions and take advantage of available tax optimization strategies.

First, it's important to understand the fundamental components of taxation systems. Taxes are typically levied by federal, state, and local governments to generate revenue. The specific tax rates and regulations vary depending on your jurisdiction.

There are different types of taxes, including income tax, sales tax, property tax, and more. Income tax is one of the most significant taxes for individuals, as it directly affects their take-home pay. It is imposed on the income earned by individuals from various sources such as wages, salaries, investments, and self-employment.

Understanding your tax bracket is crucial in determining how much of your income is subject to taxation. Tax brackets are progressive, meaning that higher-income earners are taxed at a higher rate. Familiarizing yourself with the tax brackets applicable to your income level will enable you to anticipate your tax liabilities accurately.

Additionally, deductions, credits, and exemptions can help reduce your taxable income and potentially lower your overall tax burden. Deductions are expenses that can be subtracted from your taxable income, such as mortgage interest or charitable donations. Credits provide a direct reduction in the amount of taxes owed. They can be claimed for various purposes like education or energy efficiency improvements. Exemptions allow you to exclude a certain amount of income from taxation for yourself and your dependents.

Tax planning throughout the year is essential for optimizing your returns or refunds. By strategically managing deductible expenses and utilizing tax-advantaged accounts like Health Savings Accounts (HSAs) or Flexible Spending Accounts (FSAs), you can minimize your taxable income and maximize deductions or credits available to you.

Lastly, staying informed about changes in tax laws is critical to ensure compliance and optimize your financial strategies. Tax laws may undergo revisions periodically, and being aware of these changes will allow you to adapt and make adjustments accordingly.

13.2 Common Tax Deductions, Credits, and Exemptions Available to Individuals

When it comes to managing your personal finances, understanding the basics of taxation systems is crucial. One aspect that can significantly impact your overall tax liability is taking advantage of common tax deductions, credits, and exemptions available to individuals. Utilizing these opportunities can optimize your tax returns or minimize your taxable income.

Tax deductions are expenses or amounts that are subtracted from your gross income, reducing the amount of income that is subject to tax. Here are some common deductions.

Home mortgage interest deduction: If you own a home and have a mortgage, you can deduct the interest paid on your mortgage from your taxable income. This deduction can be significant, especially in the early years of your mortgage when interest payments are higher.

State and local taxes deduction: You can deduct the amount you pay in state and local taxes from your federal taxable income. This includes income taxes, property taxes, and sales taxes.

Medical expenses deduction: If your medical expenses exceed a certain percentage of your adjusted gross income (AGI), you can deduct them from your taxable income. This can include costs such as health insurance premiums, prescription medications, doctor visits, and hospital bills.

Charitable contributions deduction: Donations made to qualified charitable organizations are deductible if you itemize deductions on your tax return. Keep in mind that there are specific rules and limitations regarding the type of donations that qualify for a deduction.

Tax credits, on the other hand, directly reduce the amount of tax you owe rather than reducing taxable income. Here are some common tax credits available to individuals.

Child Tax Credit: If you have dependent children under the age of 17, you may be eligible for a tax credit. The credit reduces your tax liability dollar-for-dollar.

Earned Income Tax Credit (EITC): This credit is designed to assist low-to-moderate-income individuals and families. The amount of credit varies based on factors such as income and family size.

Education Tax Credits: The American Opportunity Credit

and the Lifetime Learning Credit are two main education-related tax credits. These credits provide financial assistance for qualified education expenses incurred by you or your dependents.

It's essential to understand that the availability and specifics of tax deductions, credits, and exemptions may vary depending on your individual circumstances and any changes in tax laws. To ensure you take full advantage of these opportunities and maximize your tax savings, consider consulting with a certified public accountant or a tax professional who can provide personalized guidance based on your situation.

Being aware of common tax deductions, credits, and exemptions can significantly impact your overall tax liability and financial well-being. By understanding these opportunities and incorporating them into your tax planning strategy, you can effectively optimize your returns or minimize your taxable income. Remember to stay informed about any changes in tax laws and consult with professionals for personalized advice.

13.3 Utilizing Tax-advantaged Accounts to Minimize Taxable Income

One of the most effective strategies for minimizing taxable income is leveraging tax-advantaged accounts. These accounts offer unique benefits and can play a crucial role in optimizing your overall tax situation.

Health Savings Accounts (HSAs) are an excellent example of a tax-advantaged account that can benefit both your financial health and physical health. HSAs are designed to help individuals with high-deductible health insurance plans cover medical expenses. By contributing to an HSA, you can enjoy several tax advantages.

Firstly, contributions to an HSA are tax-deductible, meaning that the amount you contribute is subtracted from your taxable income. This can lower your overall tax liability and put more money back in your pocket. Additionally, any interest or investment gains earned within the HSA are also tax-free as long as they are used for qualified medical expenses.

Another type of tax-advantaged account is a Flexible Spending Account (FSA). FSAs are typically offered through employers and allow employees to set aside pre-tax dollars to pay for eligible medical expenses. Like HSAs, contributions made to an FSA reduce your taxable income, resulting in immediate tax savings. However, unlike HSAs, FSAs have a "use it or lose it" provision, meaning that any funds not used within the plan year may be forfeited.

Apart from health-related accounts, there are other tax-advantaged options available depending on your individual circumstances. For instance, if you are saving for retirement, contributing to a Traditional Individual Retirement Account (IRA) can provide significant tax benefits. When you contribute to a Traditional IRA, the contribution amount is deducted from your taxable income for the year. This effectively reduces the amount of tax you owe on that income.

On the other hand, if you qualify based on income limits, a Roth

IRA may be a favorable option. Although contributions to a Roth IRA are not tax-deductible, any earnings and withdrawals made in retirement are entirely tax-free. This presents a unique opportunity for individuals who anticipate being in a higher tax bracket during retirement.

Furthermore, other tax-advantaged accounts include 529 plans for education savings and Coverdell Education Savings Accounts (ESAs). Both these options offer tax-free growth and withdrawals when used for qualified education expenses.

Understanding the specific rules and limitations associated with each type of tax-advantaged account is essential. Familiarize yourself with contribution limits, eligibility requirements, and any restrictions on how the funds can be used. By utilizing these accounts strategically, you can potentially save a significant amount on your annual tax bill while simultaneously working towards your financial goals.

Before making any decisions about contributing to tax-advantaged accounts, consult with a financial advisor or tax professional who can provide personalized guidance based on your individual circumstances. They can help you evaluate which accounts align best with your goals and provide insights into how they fit within your overall financial plan.

In summary, tax-advantaged accounts offer valuable opportunities to minimize your taxable income and maximize your savings potential. Whether it's leveraging an HSA for medical expenses or taking advantage of retirement-focused accounts like Traditional or Roth IRAs, understanding these options can significantly impact your financial well-being. With careful planning and utilization of these accounts, you can optimize your tax situation and keep more money in your pocket for future financial growth.

13.4 Tax Planning Strategies Throughout the Year to Optimize Returns/Refunds

Tax season can often be a stressful time for many individuals, but with proper tax planning strategies, you can optimize your returns or refunds and minimize any potential financial burdens.

One important strategy is regularly reviewing and adjusting your tax withholding throughout the year. Completing a W-4 form with your employer ensures that the correct amount of taxes is being withheld from your paycheck. This prevents you from owing a large sum at tax time or receiving a significant refund, which essentially means you have been overpaying throughout the year. Adjusting your withholding based on changes in your income or family status can help align your tax obligations with your actual financial situation.

Another effective tax planning strategy is to take advantage of all eligible deductions and credits. Deductions reduce your taxable income, while credits directly reduce the amount of tax you owe. Some common deductions include mortgage interest, student loan interest, medical expenses, and certain business expenses. Tax credits, such as the Child or Earned Income Tax Credit, can lower your tax bill even further. Researching and understanding the available deductions and credits can significantly impact your overall tax liability.

Timing is also crucial when it comes to tax planning. Certain expenses can be strategically timed to maximize their tax benefits. For example, suppose you know you will have a significant medical expense in one year. In that case, you can plan it so that it falls in a year when you expect to have a higher taxable income. This way, the medical expenses can be deducted at a higher tax rate, providing more substantial tax savings.

Investing in tax-advantaged accounts can also be an effective tax planning strategy. Contributing to retirement accounts like traditional IRAs or 401(k)s not only helps secure your future but can also provide immediate tax benefits. These contributions are often tax-deductible, meaning they reduce your taxable income for the year. Additionally, funds within these accounts grow tax-deferred until withdrawal, allowing for potential long-term growth without immediate tax consequences.

Charitable giving is another avenue for tax planning. Donating to qualified charitable organizations allows you to support causes you believe in and can also provide valuable tax deductions. Keep records and receipts for all charitable donations; these documents will be essential when filing your taxes.

Last but not least, staying informed about changes in tax laws is crucial for effective tax planning. Tax laws evolve over time, and new regulations may offer additional opportunities for deductions or credits. Regularly review updates on taxation and consult with professionals if necessary to ensure that you are making informed decisions based on current regulations.

13.5 Hiring Professionals or Using Tax Software for Accurate Filing

When it comes to filing your taxes accurately and effectively, you have two main options: hiring a professional tax preparer or utilizing tax software or tools. Each option has its own advantages and considerations, so let's compare both to help you make an informed decision.

Hiring a Professional Tax Preparer

Hiring a professional tax preparer can provide several benefits, especially if you have a complex financial situation or are not confident in your ability to navigate the tax code. Here are some key advantages:

- **Expertise and knowledge:** Professional tax preparers are well-versed in tax laws, regulations, and changes. They stay updated with current tax codes and can ensure you maximize your deductions while minimizing errors.
- **Time-saving:** Managing your finances and tax preparation can be time-consuming, especially when juggling multiple responsibilities. Outsourcing this task to a professional frees up valuable time to focus on other aspects of your life.
- **Peace of mind:** Tax professionals relieve the burden by assuming the responsibility of accurately completing your tax return. This provides peace of mind, knowing that your taxes are being handled by someone experienced and knowledgeable.

However, there are a few considerations to keep in mind:

- **Cost:** Hiring a tax professional can come with a cost. The fees vary depending on the complexity of your taxes and the level of expertise required. Consider whether the potential benefits outweigh the financial investment.
- **Communication and trust:** It's crucial to communicate openly with your tax preparer and provide them with all the necessary information. Trust is also essential, as you'll disclose sensitive financial details to them.

Utilizing Tax Software

With technological advancements, numerous tax software programs and tools are available to simplify the process of filing your taxes. Here are the advantages of using tax software:

- **Affordability:** Most tax software programs provide cost-effective solutions compared to hiring a professional tax preparer. Depending on the complexity of your taxes, you typically pay a one-time fee or a subscription fee.
- **Ease of use:** Tax software is designed to guide you through each step of the tax filing process, ensuring you don't miss any important deductions or credits. These programs often include helpful resources and tips along the way.
- **Accuracy:** Tax software utilizes built-in calculations and error-checking features, reducing the likelihood of mistakes on your return. This can help minimize the risk of triggering an audit or facing penalties.

However, it's essential to consider these factors:

- **Complexity of your taxes:** While most tax software pro-grams cater to individuals with straightforward tax situations, they may not be suitable for those with complex financial circumstances. Evaluate whether the software can handle your specific needs.
- **Comfort with technology:** Using tax software requires a certain level of comfort and familiarity with technology. If you struggle with navigating digital platforms or prefer face-to-face interactions, hiring a professional might be better for you.

Whether you choose to hire a professional tax preparer or utilize tax software/tools depends on your preferences, financial situation, and comfort level with taxes. Remember that regardless of the option you select, it's essential to maintain accuracy and compliance with tax regulations.

As always, consult with trusted sources or professionals before making significant financial decisions related to taxes.

13.6 Staying informed about changes in tax laws that may affect your finances

As a responsible taxpayer, staying current with any changes in tax laws and regulations that could impact your financial situation is essential. Tax laws are constantly evolving, and staying informed about these changes can help you make smart financial decisions and optimize your tax strategy.

One way to stay informed is to regularly read reliable sources of tax information, such as government websites and tax publications, or consult with a tax professional. These sources provide valuable insights into new legislative developments, updates on deductions and credits, and any changes that may affect the way you file your taxes.

Additionally, attending seminars or webinars on tax-related topics can be a great way to deepen your understanding of intricate tax laws. Many organizations and financial institutions offer these educational opportunities to help individuals navigate the complex world of taxes.

Another effective way to stay informed about tax law changes is by subscribing to newsletters or email updates from reputable financial institutions or tax authorities. These newsletters often provide summaries of important changes in tax laws and offer practical advice on how to adapt your financial strategy accordingly.

Taking advantage of online resources can also be beneficial. There are numerous websites that provide comprehensive guides, calculators, and tools to help you understand and comply with the latest tax regulations. These resources can simplify the process of keeping up with tax law changes and enable you to make informed decisions when it comes to your finances.

It is important to note that tax laws can vary depending on your jurisdiction. Therefore, focusing on information specific to your country or region is crucial. This ensures that you are following the correct guidelines and maximizing your benefits within the legal framework.

13.7 Wrapping It Up

In this chapter, we have delved into the world of taxes and explored various strategies to optimize our financial growth through tax planning. From understanding the basics of taxation systems to utilizing tax-advantaged accounts, we have equipped ourselves with the knowledge and tools necessary to navigate the complex world of taxes.

One key takeaway from this chapter is the importance of staying informed about changes in tax laws that may affect our finances. The tax landscape is constantly evolving, and it is crucial for us to stay up to date with any new regulations or deductions that could impact our tax returns. By being proactive and staying informed, we can ensure that we take full advantage of all available tax benefits.

We have also learned the value of hiring professionals or using tax software/tools for accurate filing. Taxes can be complicated, and it is easy to make mistakes that could cost us money or even result in penalties. Seeking professional help or utilizing reliable software can help us navigate the intricacies of tax preparation and ensure that our returns are filed correctly.

Throughout this chapter, we have emphasized the importance of tax optimization as a means of maximizing our financial growth. By strategically planning our taxes throughout the year, we can minimize taxable income and potentially increase our returns or refunds. This proactive approach to tax planning can greatly contribute to our overall financial success.

As we wrap up this chapter on taxes, it is crucial to remember that taxes are an inevitable part of life. They play a significant role in shaping our financial situation and should not be overlooked or neglected. By understanding the basics of taxation systems, utilizing available deductions and credits, and staying informed about changes in tax laws, we can optimize our tax situation and set ourselves up for financial growth.

In the next chapter, we will focus on setting financial goals for different life stages. We will explore the unique considerations and challenges faced during various milestones in life, such as early adulthood, major life events, mid-life responsibilities, retirement, and later years. By understanding how our financial goals change throughout different stages of life, we can better plan for the future and ensure long-term financial security.

Chapter 14: Setting Financial Goals for Life Stages

"By failing to prepare, you are preparing to fail." – *Benjamin Franklin*

As we journey through life, our financial needs and responsibilities evolve with each passing stage. From the early years of adulthood, where we embark on educational pursuits and establish our careers, to major life events like marriage, starting a family, and eventually reaching retirement age, it is crucial to have a clear roadmap for our financial well-being. In this chapter, we will explain the importance of setting financial goals at different life stages and how they contribute to long-term financial security.

14.1 Financial Considerations During Early Adulthood

This is a crucial time when individuals are transitioning from being dependents to becoming financially independent. Whether you are just starting college or embarking on a new career, it is important to lay a solid foundation for your financial future.

During this period, many young adults face significant financial decisions, such as choosing a college or vocational school, taking out student loans, and managing expenses while pursuing education. Navigating these choices can be overwhelming, especially when trying to balance financial responsibility with personal aspirations.

Through the following case studies and real-life examples, we will highlight the experiences of young adults who have successfully navigated these early financial challenges. Their stories will provide you with inspiration and practical insights into how to make smart financial choices during this critical phase of life.

College Education Expenses

Sarah, a recent high school graduate, dreams of pursuing a college education. However, she is concerned about the financial burden it may bring. To make an informed decision, Sarah meticulously researches potential colleges, comparing tuition fees, scholarships, and financial aid packages. She also explores alternative options, such as community college or online courses, which can be more cost-effective while still providing valuable education. By carefully considering her financial situation and exploring various avenues, Sarah successfully balances her desire for higher education with her long-term financial goals.

Managing Student Loans

Michael recently graduated from college and has student loan debt that he needs to tackle. Before entering repayment, he thoroughly understands his loan terms and repayment options. Realizing the importance of staying on top of his finances, Michael creates a budget to allocate a portion of his income toward loan payments without compromising his other financial responsibilities. Michael sets himself on a path toward financial freedom by taking proactive steps and actively managing his student loans.

Starting a Career

Emily has just landed her first job after completing her degree. While excited about the opportunity, she faces the challenge of managing her newfound income responsibly. Emily created a detailed budget outlining her monthly expenses, including rent, utilities, transportation costs, and savings goals. By tracking her spending and diligently following her budget, Emily avoids falling into the temptation of overspending and ensures that she can meet her financial obligations while still enjoying her hard-earned money.

Emergency Savings

David, fresh out of college, learns the importance of building an emergency fund through personal experience. When unexpected car repairs arise, David is relieved knowing he has funds set aside for emergencies. Without this financial cushion, he might have been forced to rely on credit cards or borrow money from others, which could have created additional financial stress. David's experience highlights the value of establishing an emergency fund early on to weather unexpected financial storms.

Investing in Retirement

Ashley understands the significance of saving for retirement early in her career. Despite being in her twenties, she recognizes that time is one of her greatest assets when it comes to investing for the future. Ashley enrolls in her employer's retirement plan and takes full advantage of any matching contributions offered. Additionally, she educates herself about different investment options available within the plan to ensure her retirement savings grow steadily over time. By prioritizing retirement savings at a young age, Ashley sets herself up for a secure and comfortable future.

Building Credit Responsibly

Daniel recognizes the need to establish good credit early in his adulthood to qualify for future loans or housing opportunities. He starts by obtaining a credit card with a low limit. He uses it responsibly by making small purchases and paying off the balance in full each month. Daniel also monitors his credit report regularly to identify any inaccuracies or fraudulent activity. Through diligent credit management practices, Daniel builds a solid credit history that opens doors to favorable interest rates and greater financial flexibility.

These case studies and real-life examples illustrate the various financial considerations individuals face in their early adult-hood. By understanding these scenarios and learning from others' experiences, readers can gain valuable insights into effectively managing their finances during this critical phase of life.

14.2 Navigating Finances During Major Life Events: Marriage, Having Children

Life is a series of beautiful milestones, and each milestone often comes with its own financial considerations. One of the most significant life events that can profoundly impact your finances is getting married and starting a family. While love may be the foundation of a successful marriage, it is essential to also build a solid financial foundation to support your shared dreams and aspirations.

When two individuals join their lives together in matrimony, aligning their financial goals and priorities becomes crucial. Open and honest communication about money is key to main-taining a healthy relationship. Take the time to sit down with your partner and have an open discussion about your individual financial situation, including income, assets, debts, and spending habits.

Once you have a clear understanding of each other's financial standing, it is essential to establish shared financial goals as a couple. Discuss your long-term aspirations, such as homeownership, early retirement, or children's education, and create a plan to achieve them together. By setting common objectives, you can work towards them as a team, supporting and motivating each other along the way.

As you embark on this journey together, it is crucial to consider the financial implications of having children. Raising a child requires careful planning and budgeting to ensure their well-being while maintaining financial stability. Start by estimating the costs associated with childbirth, such as medical expenses, prenatal care, and delivery costs. Additionally, factor in ongoing expenses like diapers, formula, clothing, healthcare, and education.

To financially prepare for a child's arrival, it is advisable to create an emergency fund specifically earmarked for childcare expenses. This fund will provide a safety net during unexpected circumstances or emergencies. It is recommended to save at least three to six months' worth of living expenses to ensure you are adequately prepared for any unforeseen events.

Another important consideration when starting a family is reviewing your health insurance coverage. Evaluate your current policy to determine if it will adequately cover maternity costs and pediatric care. Consider adding or adjusting coverage options if necessary to ensure comprehensive coverage for both the mother and the child.

Additionally, take advantage of government programs or employer benefits that support growing families. Research available tax credits or deductions related to having children, such as the Child Tax Credit or the Dependent Care Flexible Spending Account (FSA). These programs can help alleviate some of the financial burden associated with raising children.

As you navigate through major life events like marriage and having children, it is crucial to continuously evaluate and adjust your financial plan. Regularly revisit your budget and make necessary modifications based on changing circumstances or new goals. Remember that flexibility and adaptability are key components of successful financial management.

While embarking on this new chapter in your life may seem overwhelming at times, remember that with proper planning and open communication, you can navigate these financial waters successfully. Seek advice from financial professionals if needed, and continue educating yourself about personal finance topics relevant to your situation.

14.3 Planning for Mid-Life Responsibilities: Buying a Home and Supporting Aging Parents

As we navigate through different stages of life, our financial goals and responsibilities evolve. In our mid-life years, two significant financial considerations often come into play: buying a home and supporting aging parents. These milestones bring unique challenges and require careful planning to ensure financial stability and security.

Buying a Home

Owning a home is a milestone that many people aspire to achieve in their mid-life years. It provides stability, a sense of ownership, and the potential for long-term financial growth. However, purchasing a home is a major financial decision that should be approached with careful consideration.

Here are some key steps involved in buying a home.

- **Assessing your financial readiness:** Before diving into the home-buying process, evaluating your financial situation is crucial. This includes reviewing your credit score, saving for a down payment, and considering the additional costs associated with homeownership, such as property taxes and maintenance expenses.
- **Setting a budget:** Analyze your income, existing debt obligations, and monthly expenses to determine how much you can comfortably afford to spend on housing. This will help you establish a realistic budget and avoid overextending yourself financially.
- **Researching the housing market:** Gain familiarity with the local real estate market to understand property prices, neighborhoods, and trends. This knowledge will empower you to make informed decisions when selecting the right home for your needs and budget.
- **Obtaining mortgage financing:** Explore different mortgage options and compare interest rates, terms, and loan features. Consulting with a mortgage professional will ensure you choose the most suitable financing option for your circumstances.
- **Conducting thorough inspections:** Once you find a

prospective home, it's crucial to conduct thorough inspections to identify any potential issues or hidden costs. This may involve hiring professionals to assess the property's condition, including its structural integrity, plumbing, electrical systems, etc.

Negotiating offers and closing the deal: Skillful negotiation can help you secure the best price for your dream home. Understanding the art of negotiation and working closely with your real estate agent will increase your chances of success. Finally, completing the necessary paperwork and legal requirements will finalize the purchase.

Supporting Aging Parents

The mid-life years often coincide with the stage of life when our parents are getting older and may require additional support. As their children, it becomes our responsibility to ensure their well-being while managing our own financial obligations.

Here are some essential aspects to consider when supporting aging parents.

- **Open communication:** It is crucial to initiate open and honest conversations with your parents about their financial situation. Discuss their retirement savings, healthcare needs, and any potential long-term care plans they may have in place.
- **Understanding resources and benefits:** Research government programs, insurance coverage, and community

resources that can provide support for elderly individuals. Familiarize yourself with available options so that you can assist your parents in accessing the services they need.

· **Creating a caregiving plan:** Collaborate with siblings or other family members to develop a caregiving plan that outlines responsibilities, financial contributions, and the division of tasks. By sharing the caregiving load, you can alleviate some of the financial burdens associated with caring for aging parents.

· **Long-term care insurance:** Consider exploring long-term care insurance options for your parents as a means to manage potential expenses related to healthcare services or assisted living facilities in the future.

· **Estate planning:** Encourage your parents to create or update their estate plans, including wills, powers of attorney, and healthcare directives. This preparation ensures their wishes are known and respected while minimizing potential legal complications down the road.

Through diligent planning and decision-making in these areas, we can ensure a more secure financial future for ourselves and our loved ones during this significant phase of life.

14.4 Preparing for Retirement: Saving Habits and Investment Strategies

As you approach the later stages of your life, it becomes increasingly important to start preparing for retirement. We've talked about retirement planning in Chapter 12. By developing good saving habits and implementing effective investment strategies, you can lay a solid foundation for your future.

As you near retirement, it's important to transition from the accumulation phase, where you focus on saving, to the distribution phase, where you start utilizing your savings.

In the later stages of life, financial planning extends beyond personal needs. It involves considerations related to inheritance and legacy planning. Properly managing your assets and planning for the future can leave a lasting legacy for your loved ones while minimizing potential tax implications.

14.5 Adjustments to Finances and Legacy Planning in Later Years

As life continues to unfold, it is essential to continuously reassess and adjust your financial goals. This may include revisiting your investment strategies, reevaluating your risk tolerance, and adapting your estate planning based on changing circumstances. You can ensure your financial well-being throughout your later years by remaining proactive and flexible.

Lastly, as you contemplate your finances in later years, it's important to consider legacy planning. You may want to leave behind a meaningful legacy for future generations or donate to charitable causes close to your heart. Developing a comprehensive plan that addresses your wishes for wealth transfer or philanthropic endeavors will allow you to shape the impact you have even after you've passed.

You can confidently navigate the financial landscape in later years through careful consideration and strategic adjustments. By proactively addressing retirement planning, maximizing contributions, adjusting goals, and considering legacy planning, you'll be well-prepared for the next chapter of your financial journey.

14.6 Wrapping It Up

In this chapter, we have explored the importance of setting financial goals for different life stages. From early adulthood to retirement and beyond, each stage presents unique challenges and opportunities for financial growth. By understanding these considerations and taking proactive steps to manage our finances, we can secure a brighter future for ourselves and our loved ones.

Chapter 15: Taking Control of Your Financial Future

"Your financial future is not defined by your circumstances, but by the choices you make today."

Your financial future – now that's a canvas waiting for your brushstrokes. It's easy to think that circumstances hold the power to shape it, but the real magic lies in the choices you make today. Your decisions are the architects of the skyscrapers or the humble cottages in your financial skyline.

Circumstances might be the backdrop, but they don't dictate the plot. Your choices and your actions determine the narrative of your financial journey. When facing challenges, make choices that turn them into stepping stones, not stumbling blocks. Embrace opportunities, even if they come disguised as obstacles.

Every dollar you save, every investment you make, and every financial habit you cultivate are the seeds for a prosperous tomorrow. It's not about where you start but the direction you're heading. Your financial future is a culmination of the choices you make, the habits you build, and the goals you set.

Throughout this book, we have explored the essential principles and strategies for mastering personal finance. We have delved into the importance of financial literacy in today's world and debunked common misconceptions that may hinder our progress. We have uncovered the profound impact of personal finance on our overall well-being and provided guidance on overcoming fears and gaining confidence in managing money.

In this final chapter, we will recapitulate the key concepts covered throughout the book, reinforcing their importance and providing practical steps for immediate action.

But before we proceed, take a moment to reflect on how far you've come. Consider the goals you initially set for yourself, whether it was paying off debt, saving for a down payment on a home, or preparing for retirement. Recognize your progress and acknowledge the determination and resilience that brought you here.

Remember, it is never too late to start taking control of your financial future. The journey may be challenging at times, but with persistence and determination, you will overcome any obstacles in your path. Your financial freedom awaits; seize it with both hands and create the life you deserve.

15.1 Take Immediate Action towards Financial Empowerment

Now that you have gained a wealth of knowledge about personal finance and money management, it is time to take action and begin your journey toward financial empowerment. This book has provided the tools and strategies necessary to make informed financial decisions. Now, it is up to you to put them into practice.

Taking control of your financial future begins with a mindset shift. Understand that you have the power to shape your financial destiny and that every small step you take toward financial literacy and responsibility will significantly impact you in the long run. It may feel overwhelming at first, but remember that even the smallest of actions can lead to substantial results over time.

Start by setting clear and specific financial goals for yourself. Whether you're saving for a down payment on a house, paying off debt, or building a retirement fund, having defined objectives will give you something to strive toward. Break these goals down into smaller, manageable tasks and create a timeline for achieving them. This will not only help you stay focused but also provide a sense of accomplishment as you tick off each milestone along the way.

It is important to remember that financial empowerment is an ongoing process. Like any other skill, mastering money management takes time, practice, and continuous learning. Stay committed to improving your financial literacy by staying informed about current trends and changes in laws that may impact your finances. Seek additional resources such as books, websites, and tools to further enhance your knowledge and provide practical guidance.

Don't be afraid to seek help when needed. Financial advisors, mentors, and support groups can offer invaluable advice and guidance as you navigate your personal finance journey. Surround yourself with individuals who share similar financial goals and aspirations, as they can provide motivation and accountability throughout your journey.

Lastly, remember that personal finance is not just about numbers and spreadsheets; it is about aligning your financial decisions with your values and priorities. Take the time to reflect on what truly matters to you and how your finances can support those aspirations. By incorporating your values into your financial decisions, you will find more fulfillment and satisfaction in achieving your goals.

So, I encourage you to take immediate action today. Start implementing the lessons you have learned from this book and embrace the opportunities that come with financial empowerment. With dedication, perseverance, and a commitment to lifelong learning, you have the power to master money skills and shape a prosperous future for yourself. Good luck on your journey towards financial independence!

15.2 Reinforcing the Importance of Ongoing Financial Education

Throughout this book, we've covered a wide range of personal finance topics, providing you with the essential knowledge and skills to take control of your financial future. But remember, learning about personal finance is not a one-time event. It's an ongoing process that requires continuous education and adaptation to keep up with ever-changing economic conditions.

Financial trends and regulations evolve rapidly in today's fast-paced world, and staying informed is crucial. By making a commitment to lifelong learning, you can ensure that you are always equipped with the latest information and strategies to make smart financial decisions.

But why is ongoing financial education so important? Firstly, it helps you stay ahead of the curve. By staying informed about changes in tax laws, investment opportunities, or insurance policies, you can proactively adjust your financial plans to maximize your wealth-building potential.

Secondly, ongoing financial education empowers you to make informed decisions. With a solid understanding of personal finance concepts, you can critically evaluate financial products and services and choose the ones that align with your goals and values. This knowledge protects you from falling prey to scams or making impulsive decisions.

Additionally, ongoing financial education allows you to adapt your financial strategies to different life stages. As you progress through different phases in life—such as starting a family, buying a home, or preparing for retirement—you will encounter new opportunities and challenges. Continuous learning equips you with the tools needed to navigate these transitions successfully.

So, how can you continue your financial education? There are several avenues.

Books and websites: Continuously seek out reputable sources of information on personal finance. Look for authors and websites that provide well-researched and up-to-date content. Consider joining online communities or forums where you can engage with others who share similar interests.

Workshops and seminars: Many organizations offer workshops and seminars on various personal finance topics. Take advantage of these opportunities to expand your knowledge and gain insights from experts in the field.

Professional certifications: If you want to deepen your understanding of specific areas within personal finance, consider pursuing professional certifications. These certifications provide in-depth knowledge and demonstrate your expertise in a particular aspect of personal finance.

Networking: Engage with like-minded individuals who are also committed to improving their financial literacy. Attend conferences or join local groups where you can share ideas, ask questions, and learn from others' experiences.

Podcasts and webinars: Podcasts and webinars are convenient ways to access educational content on the go. Look for podcasts or webinars that cover personal finance topics and listen to them during your commute or while doing chores.

15.3 Share Newfound Knowledge with Others

Now that you have gained a strong foundation in personal finance and have equipped yourself with the essential skills to budget and manage money wisely, it is time to consider the impact you can make in the lives of others. Sharing your knowledge and experiences with family, friends, and even strangers can have a profound ripple effect on their financial well-being.

By spreading the wisdom you have acquired through this book, you can empower others to take control of their financial future and break free from the cycle of money mismanagement. When we openly discuss personal finance, we create a supportive community where everyone can learn from each other's successes and challenges.

One way to share your knowledge is by starting conversations about personal finance with people in your life. Whether it's discussing the importance of budgeting or sharing tips on saving strategies, these conversations serve as a catalyst for change. Encourage open dialogue and create a safe space for individuals to ask questions and seek guidance.

You can also consider organizing workshops or seminars within your community. These events provide a platform for people to learn practical money skills and gain insight into financial planning. By offering your expertise and guidance, you can help individuals take their first steps toward financial independence.

Additionally, advocating for financial literacy education in schools and organizations is another way to make a lasting impact. By raising awareness about the importance of teaching personal finance at an early age, you can contribute to a future where everyone has access to the knowledge and tools necessary for financial success.

Remember, each person you educate and inspire becomes another link in the chain of financial empowerment. As more individuals gain control over their finances, our society benefits from increased stability, resilience, and prosperity.

So, seize this opportunity to be an agent of change. Share your insights, experiences, and newfound knowledge with others. Together, let's create a world where everyone can master money skills and achieve financial well-being.

Finally, I urge you to share this book with others who could benefit from its valuable insights. By becoming an advocate for financial literacy and empowering those around you, you contribute to a society that thrives economically and emotionally.

15.4 Final Words of Motivation

I want to leave you with a final dose of motivation and encouragement. Throughout this book, we've explored various aspects of money management, budgeting, saving, investing, and planning for the future. You've learned valuable skills and gained a deeper understanding of navigating the complex world of personal finance.

Now, armed with knowledge and practical strategies, it's time for you to take control of your financial future. Remember, you have the power to shape your financial destiny. No matter where you are in life or what challenges you may face, there is always an opportunity to improve your financial situation.

It's important to embrace the mindset that your financial success is within reach. Believe in yourself and your ability to make positive changes. Visualize your desired future – a life free from financial stress and filled with opportunities. This vision will guide you as you work towards your goals.

But remember, achieving financial success requires action. It's not enough to simply read about personal finance concepts and strategies; you must put them into practice. Start by taking small steps toward your goals. It could be something as simple as creating a budget, automating your savings, or educating yourself further on investment opportunities.

Don't be afraid to ask for help or seek professional guidance along the way. Financial advisors, accountants, and mentors can provide valuable insights and support on your journey toward financial independence. Don't hesitate to reach out and tap into their knowledge and expertise.

Additionally, remember the importance of ongoing financial education. The world of personal finance is constantly evolving, with new trends, laws, and technologies shaping the landscape. Stay informed by reading books, following reputable websites and blogs, attending seminars or webinars, and participating in online forums.

Lastly, remember that personal finance is not just about accumulating wealth; it's about using your resources wisely to create a life of meaning and fulfillment. Money can provide security and freedom, but it should never become the sole focus of our lives. Remember to cultivate a healthy balance between financial success and other areas that bring you joy – family, relationships, health, hobbies, and personal growth.

Conclusion

In the journey of mastering personal finance, we have covered a comprehensive range of topics and strategies to help you budget and manage money wisely. Throughout this book, we have emphasized the importance of financial literacy in today's world and debunked common misconceptions about personal finance. We have explored the impact of personal finance on overall well-being and provided guidance on overcoming fears and gaining confidence in managing money.

From setting goals for financial success to taking the first steps toward financial independence, we have shown you the power of cultivating a positive financial mindset. By aligning your values with your financial goals and developing an action plan, you can prioritize your objectives and stay disciplined, consistent, and resilient in achieving financial success.

We have demonstrated that creating a budget is the foundation of financial success. By tracking income and expenses accurately, categorizing expenses, and identifying areas for improvement, you can create a realistic spending plan and set aside savings. Regularly reviewing and adjusting your budget will ensure optimal results.

Furthermore, you can identify areas of overspending or inefficiency by gaining control of your finances through effective tracking of income and expenses, organizing financial documents, utilizing technology for expense tracking, and analyzing spending patterns. Implementing strategies to reduce expenses without compromising your quality of life and developing habits for mindful spending and responsible consumption will help you develop healthy spending habits.

We have emphasized the importance of saving strategies in building a strong financial cushion. Whether setting short-term or long-term goals, choosing the right savings account or investment vehicle, automating savings, cutting expenses, or establishing emergency funds and retirement savings, saving is crucial in achieving financial stability and security.

Debt management has also been explored as part of this journey. Understanding different types of debt, assessing your debt situation, creating a repayment plan, and utilizing debt consolidation strategies are all stepping stones toward breaking free from the debt cycle. We have also highlighted the importance of maintaining good credit while repaying debt and implementing long-term strategies to avoid future debt.

Impulse buying and overspending can significantly hinder your financial progress. However, you can develop healthy spending habits by identifying triggers and underlying causes of impulsive spending, curbing impulsive buying behavior, creating a realistic spending plan aligned with your values, practicing mindful spending techniques, evaluating purchases based on value and long-term impact, and building resilience against persuasive marketing tactics.

Credit management is another key aspect covered in this book. Understanding credit scores and reports, establishing credit responsibly, managing credit cards wisely, understanding interest rates and fees, improving credit scores, and navigating credit applications, loans, and mortgages are all vital elements in becoming a responsible borrower.

We have highlighted the importance of protecting yourself and your assets through insurance coverage. By understanding different types of insurance coverage, assessing individual needs, comparing providers, ensuring adequate coverage at affordable premiums, evaluating risks, mitigating potential losses, and maximizing insurance benefits through proper claims management, you can achieve peace of mind in uncertain times.

Investing basics and real estate wealth building have been explored as avenues for growing your wealth over time. By harnessing the power of compound interest, assessing risk tolerance and investment objectives, diversifying investments to minimize risk, understanding different investment vehicles, evaluating opportunities, monitoring performance, analyzing potential returns on real estate investments, and considering property management considerations—these strategies can help you build long-term wealth.

We have emphasized retirement planning as an essential step toward securing your future. Establishing retirement goals, calculating retirement needs based on anticipated expenses, evaluating different retirement savings accounts such as IRAs and 401(k)s, maximizing contributions, and taking advantage of employer matches or retirement plans are all crucial components in ensuring a comfortable retirement.

Understanding taxes is vital in optimizing your financial growth. We have discussed taxation systems, common deductions and credits available to individuals, utilizing tax-advantaged accounts to minimize taxable income, and tax planning strategies throughout the year for optimized returns or refunds. Staying informed about changes in tax laws is equally important for efficiently handling your finances.

Financial goals evolve throughout different life stages. From early adulthood to major life events like marriage or having children to mid-life responsibilities and retirement planning to adjustments in later years, financial considerations change with circumstances. Adapting goals based on changing circumstances is crucial in maintaining financial stability.

Personal finance mastery requires dedication, education, discipline, and continuous learning. By following the step-by-step guidance provided in this book and utilizing the various strategies outlined for each aspect of personal finance—budgeting, tracking income and expenses, saving strategies, debt management, healthy spending habits, credit management, insurance protection, investing basics with an emphasis on real estate wealth building—retirement planning, tax optimization strategies—we hope to have equipped you with the necessary knowledge to navigate the complex world of personal finance successfully.

Remember that your financial future lies in your hands. You must take immediate action to become financially empowered.

You have the power to shape your financial future. Believe in yourself, take control, make wise decisions, be proactive in managing your money, track your progress regularly, adapt when needed, share your knowledge with others, continue to educate yourself, and never stop learning.

With determination and commitment to mastering personal finance skills, you can achieve financial freedom, build a secure future for yourself and your loved ones, and enjoy peace of mind knowing that you are on solid ground financially.

Go forth with confidence!

References

Money, Like Emotions, Is Something You Must Control - Unravel Mind.
   https://unravelmind.com/money-like-emotions-is-something-you-must-control/

Nicholas Hall · Speakers 2019.
   https://mosurbanforum.com/speakers/2019/nikolas_kholl/

Financial Planning.
   https://anelaevents.com/financial-planning

Unleashing the Power of Your Mind for Financial Abundance.
   https://www.donnaboylen.com/post/unleashing-the-power-of-your-mind-for-financial-abundance

25 Money Affirmations to Practice - Millennial Nextdoor.
   https://millennialnextdoor.com/money-affirmations/

Understanding the Impact of Limiting Beliefs on Personal Growth.
   https://lifecoachtraining.co/category/mindset-and-belief

215

s/understanding-the-impact-of-limiting-beliefs-on-perso
nal-growth/

Setting and Achieving Financial Milestones - Shannon J Her-
nandez - Look Well, Feel Well.
https://www.shannonjhernandez.com/setting-and-achiev
ing-financial-milestones/

Identifying Your Goals and Values.
https://www.wakeupthankful.com/setting-an-intention-f
or-the-day-identifying-your-goals-and-values

How to Prioritize Financial Goals for Optimal Personal Finance.
https://1minute.guide/2023/09/08/how-to-prioritize-fina
ncial-goals-for-optimal-personal-finance/

Navigating Financial Stress: Practical Strategies for Managing
Your Fi.
https://financialfootwork.com/blogs/my-money-blog/ho
w-to-handle-financial-stress

Financial Goals and Motivation: The Key to Achieving Financial
Success | Mr Accountants.
https://mr-accountants.com/financial-goals-and-motiva
tion-the-key-to-achieving-financial-success/

Budgeting Tips that Can Boost Your Bottom Line | Business
Allies.
https://vaallies.org/budgeting-tips-that-can-boost-your-
bottom-line/

Budgeting Strategies to Maximize Insurance Benefits
https://wealthnation.io/blog/free-budgeting-strategies/

Where Should You Look to Find Your Current Expenses When Building Your Budget? A Comprehensive Guide -.
https://customresearchpapers.biz/where-should-you-look-to-find-your-current-expenses-when-building-your-budget-a-comprehensive-guide/

How to Set Up a Family Budget – For Rent Edmonton – 911Rent.
https://911rent.ca/how-to-set-up-a-family-budget/

Mastering Home Maintenance: Budgeting, Planning, and Savings.
https://storiesofahouse.com/mastering-home-maintenance-budgeting-planning-and-savings/

5 Tips when Creating a Budget that Works for You - FixMy.lk.
https://fixmy.lk/creating-a-budget-that-works-for-you/

How to Balance Family's Financial Priorities with Your Own Personal Goals - Preggy to Mommy.
https://preggytomommy.com/how-to-balance-familys-financial-priorities/

Zig Ziglar Quote: Money isn't the most important thing in life, but it's reasonably close to oxygen on the 'gotta have it' scale..
https://www.wishafriend.com/quotes/qid/7558/

Smart Budgeting for Newlyweds: Navigating Finances Together for a Secure Future-Loan Societies.

https://www.loansocieties.com/smart-budgeting-for-new lyweds-navigating-finances-together-for-a-secure-future /

How to Make a Budget that You can Actually Stick to? - Lifeandtrendz. https://lifeandtrendz.com/lifestyle/how-to-make-a-budg et-that-you-can-actually-stick-to/

Budgeting Tools For 2023 - Rumah Metaverse. http://rumah metaverse.com/digital-startup/budgeting-tools/

5 Effective Strategies to Stick to Your Grocery Budget. https://top-10.blog/finance/5-effective-strategies-to-stic k-to-your-grocery-budget/

Saving Money on Household Goods Without Extreme Couponing. https://snipon.com/blog/saving-money-household-go ods-without-extreme-couponing/

How to Simplify and Illuminate Your Life with Voluntary Simplicity - Survival Skill Zone. https://survivalskillzone.com/how-to-simplify-and-illu minate-your-life-with-voluntary-simplicity/

Creating A Personal Budget: Managing Your Finances Effectively - Online Accounting Tips. https://onlineaccountingtips.com/creating-a-personal-b udget-managing-your-finances-effectively/

Getting A Handle On Your Personal Finances.

https://www.financeteam.net/handle-personal-finances/

Financial Planning: Building a Solid Foundation for a Bright Financial Future – Money Health Finance.
https://moneyhealthfinance.com/financial-planning-building-a-solid-foundation-for-a-bright-financial-future/

6 types of savings accounts: opportunities for growing your money - The Mad Capitalist.
https://themadcapitalist.com/types-of-savings-accounts/

The Pros and Cons of Different Savings Accounts -.
https://txhsfbgameday.com/the-pros-and-cons-of-different-savings-accounts/

Types of Saving Accounts with Various Features in 2024.
https://financedwise.com/types-of-saving-accounts-with-various-features/

How To Improve Your Finances With a High-Yield Savings Account - Global Brands Magazine.
https://www.globalbrandsmagazine.com/how-to-improve-your-finances-with-a-high-yield-savings-account/

Tips to Save $10,000 in a Year: Guide to Financial Independence.
https://insights.masterworks.com/finance/wealth-planning/save-10000-in-a-year/

The Penny Pincher's Guide to Saving and Thriving – Elect Pamela Banks.

https://electpamelabanks.com/the-penny-pinchers-guide -to-saving-and-thriving/

How Much Should I Save Each Month?. https://marxcommunications.com/how-much-should-i-s ave-each-month/

Understanding Debt Relief Options | Live Hall City. https://live hallcity.com/23197-understanding-debt-relief-options-18/

Managing Personal Debt: Strategies for Taking Control of Your Finances - Berken & Cloyes. https://berkencloyes.com/managing-personal-debt-strat egies-for-taking-control-of-your-finances/

Effective Strategies For Rapid Credit Card Debt Payoff -. https://ishratamin.com/strategies-for-paying-off-credit- card-debt-quickly/

The Impact Of Balance Transfer On Credit Score - Andromeda. https://www.andromedaloans.com/the-impact-of-balanc e-transfer-on-credit-score/

Personal Finance Planning: A 8-Step-by-Step Guide to Secure Your Financial Future - Biznesnetwork. https://www.biznesnetwork.com/2023/08/07/personal-fi nance-planning-a-8-step-by-step-guide-to-secure-your- financial-future/

5 Best Ways to Improve Your Credit Score Quickly! - Groupe Baronello.

https://groupebaronello.com/5-best-ways-to-improve-your-credit-score-quickly/

How to Use Credit Cards to Raise Your Poor Credit Rating - Washington Physicians.
https://washingtonphysicians.org/how-to-use-credit-cards-to-raise-your-poor-credit-rating/

Top 14 Impulse Buying Habits and How They Affect Your Savings.
https://dailycheddar.com/top-14-impulse-buying-habits-and-how-they-affect-your-savings/

How to Create a Budget for Your Monthly Expenses.
https://iopenusa.com/monthly-expenses/

Unlocking the Secrets of Achieving Financial Security Tips - EduQuest.
https://teachinglibrarian.org/unlocking-the-secrets-of-achieving-financial-security-tips-16823/

How To Make Credit Work For You | Key Credit Repair.
https://keycreditrepair.com/how-to-make-credit-work-for-you/

5 Things You Should Know About Your Credit Score: Insights from Mike Lombardo, Real Estate Broker in Cape Coral | The Mike Lombardo Team.
https://www.mikelom.com/blog/5-things-you-should-know-about-your-credit-score-insights-from-mike-lombardo-real-estate-broker-in-cape-coral/

What Is FICO Score Mean? - LOFTY CREDIT!LOFTY CREDIT!.
https://loftycredit.com/what-is-fico-score-mean/

Understanding Credit: Tips for Improving Your Credit Score
and Managing Debt | Vincent Camarda.
https://vincentcamarda.com/financial-planning/understa
nding-credit-tips-for-improving-your-credit-score-and-
managing-debt/

Demystifying Credit Scores A Practical Guide to Understand
and Manage Your Credit Health – Volvo Tommy.
https://volvo-tommy.com/demystifying-credit-scores-a-
practical-guide-to-understand-and-manage-your-credit-
health/

Credit Cards Unveiled: How to Maximize Benefits and Minimize
Risks | Penn Credit Corporation | Finance.
https://penncreditcorporation.org/credit-cards-unveiled-
how-to-maximize-benefits-and-minimize-risks/

How To Raise Your Credit Score 200 Points in 30 Days — The
Credit Repair Shop.
https://thecreditrepairshop.com/how-to-raise-your-cred
it-score-200-points-in-30-days/

Credit Do's and Don'ts.
https://praisecharlotte.com/2196496/credit-dos-and-don
ts/

8 Tips To Improve Your Credit Score.
https://www.homeloangurus.com/post/8-tips-to-improv

e-your-credit-score

Trader cactusanalysis — Trading Ideas & Charts — TradingView.
https://www.tradingview.com/u/cactusanalysis/

Where to Invest Money to Get Good Returns for Beginners: A Comprehensive Guide – ForexSQ.
https://www.forexsq.com/where-to-invest-money-to-get-good-returns-for-beginners-a-comprehensive-guide/

types of mutual funds - Wizard Global.
https://www.physicalshares.com/tag/types-of-mutual-funds/

Quotes by Louis J. Glickman :: Finest Quotes.
http://www.finestquotes.com/author_quotes-author-Louis+J.+Glickman-page-0.htm

Mortgage Loans with Key Facts Every Homebuyer Should Know – Halogen Records.
https://www.halogenrecords.com/mortgage-loans-with-key-facts-every-homebuyer-should-know.htm

Real Estate: Benefits of Investing in Rental Properties.
https://www.harrowteam.com/post/real-estate-benefits-of-investing-in-rental-properties

Let's Explore 10 Lucrative Non-Traditional Investment Options - Moneyadviceblog.
https://www.moneyadviceblog.net/lets-explore-10-lucrat

ive-non-traditional-investment-options/

The Benefits of a 401(k) And IRA - The Noodle Box.
   https://thenoodlebox.net/personal-finance/benefits-401k
-ira/

How an Employer's 401(k) Match Can Help Secure Your Retir-
ment.
   https://www.clayfinancial.com/blog/the-importance-of-l
everaging-your-employers-401k-match-for-a-secure-reti

Benefits Received Rule Definition. – InfoComm.
   https://www.infocomm.ky/benefits-received-rule-definiti
on/

Aron Govil shares 24 Tax Deductions Your Small Business May
Be Missing.
   https://arongovilgiving.com/aron-govil-shares-24-tax-d
eductions-your-small-business-may-be-missing-out-on/

How Retirement Account Withdrawals Affect Your Social Security Taxes.
   https://socialsecurityofficesnearme.com/taxes-social-sec
urity/how-retirement-account-withdrawals-affect-your-s
ocial-security-taxes/

Maximizing Your Tax Efficiency: Strategies and Tips for Opti-
mizing Income Tax Returns | SemiOffice.Com.
   https://semioffice.com/business-entrepreneurship/maxi
mizing-your-tax-efficiency-strategies-and-tips-for-optim
izing-income-tax-returns/

"Ed Board Needs Better Plan." The Hutchinson News, vol. , no. , 2015, p. n/a.

Financial Planning: "How do I support my aging parents, pay my bills, and save for the future?" | Wealth-Building Made Simple.
https://askphillip.phillipwashingtonjr.com/e/financial-pla nning-how-do-i-support-my-aging-parents-pay-my-bill s-and-save-for-the-future/

Made in the USA
Middletown, DE
02 September 2024